Teach Yourself Crochet Ribbon Accents

Lisa Gentry

Ribbon is exciting to look at, wonderfully textured to the touch—why not learn some new ways to add it to your crochet projects? Better yet, you can make an entire necklace, scarf, or shawl out of beautiful ribbon yarn! Lisa Gentry's newest designs feature her ribbon crochet techniques, yielding creations that will tantalize your imagination. Treat yourself to the fun of fashioning eleven garments and accessories with the beauty of ribbon!

Cutting THE RIBBON ON A NEW TECHNIQUE

"I had tons of ribbon yarn on hand," says Lisa Gentry. "I was just imagining what could be done with ribbon when I realized you could crochet it directly onto a project. I introduced the idea to the women who take my knit and crochet classes. They were so excited! It was wonderful to hear them say, 'I can do that!'"

As a designer of crochet and knitting patterns, Lisa is always finding new ways to improve or embellish those arts. Many fans of crochet know Lisa Gentry as the Guinness Book of Records Fastest Crocheter. She's also America's fastest knitter, currently holding that title with the Craft Yarn Council of America.

Lisa grew up in Germany and now lives in Louisiana with her husband. Although she was recently invited to appear on local television to showcase her skills, Lisa regretfully refused. "I'm putting all my time into designing for books right now, and I'm thrilled about this book on using ribbon yarn. I think all women love ribbons and will enjoy this new way to use them."

To find more of Lisa Gentry's innovative techniques and exciting patterns, visit www.leisurearts.com.

I0894097

LEISURE ARTS, INC.
Little Rock, Arkansas

Embellishing WITH RIBBON

Ribbon makes a great accent for your crochet projects, from a purse and clothing to an afghan with a variety of things in between. Use ribbon along with size 5 thread to make a lacy lattice with flowers or simply join ribbon to your crochet project to create ruffles. Even add ribbon flowers for a lovely trim. You don't have to stop here, either. Use these techniques to embellish all of your favorite crochet patterns.

DIFFERENT *Types* OF RIBBON

1 RIBBON YARNS

There are numerous ribbon yarns to choose from. They are made by yarn companies and are just perfect for crocheting, since they're not stiff and therefore drape well. The style of ribbon yarn used in a project can depend on the technique being used. Some techniques require a ribbon with ready-made holes like the checkerboard, the railroad, and the lacy ladder styles. Other ribbon yarns are solid, but loosely woven, so a crochet hook can easily be inserted into them. Refer to the project that you're making for the suggested ribbon yarn type.

checkerboard

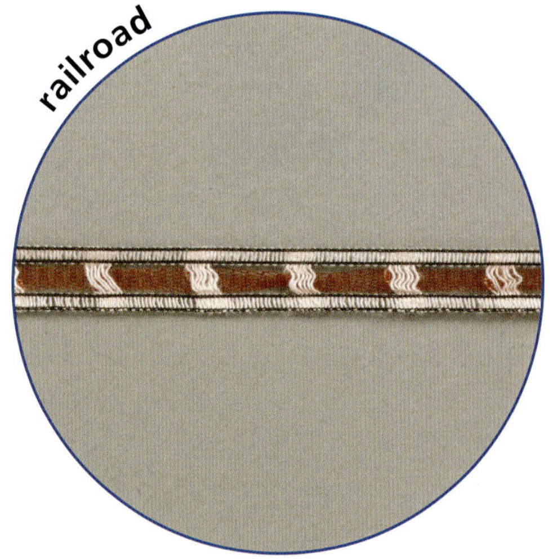
railroad

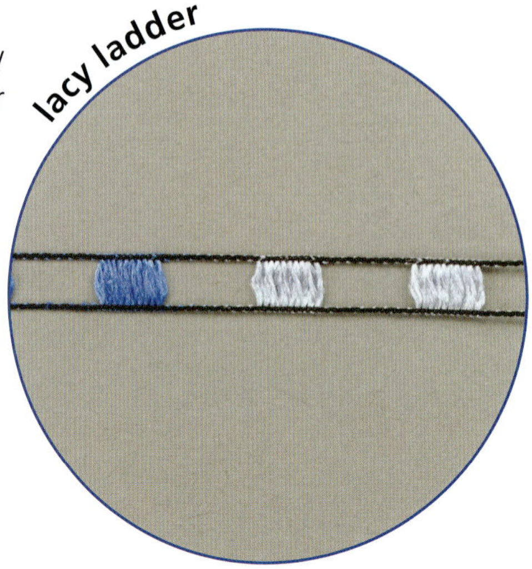
lacy ladder

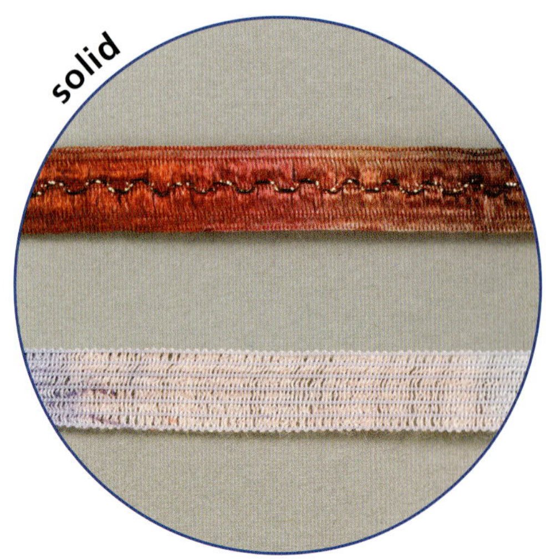
solid

2 WOVEN EDGED RIBBONS

Woven edged ribbons are made by ribbon companies. They are woven on a loom, giving them finished selvedges or edges, and making them suitable for attaching to crochet projects. They come on spools in different widths with limited yardage. The Bolero is made with a medium width ribbon and the Purse is made with a wide width ribbon.

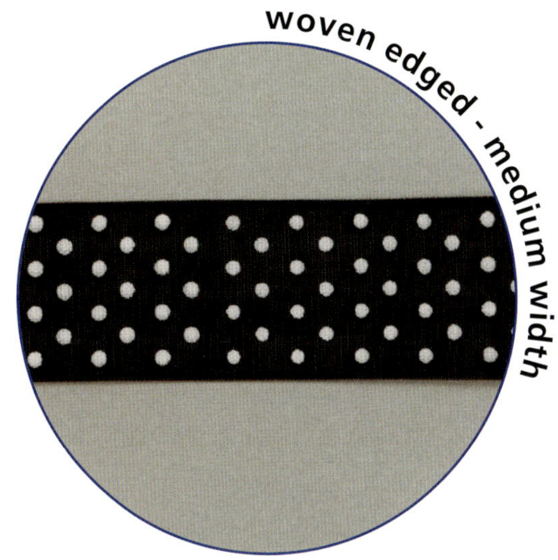

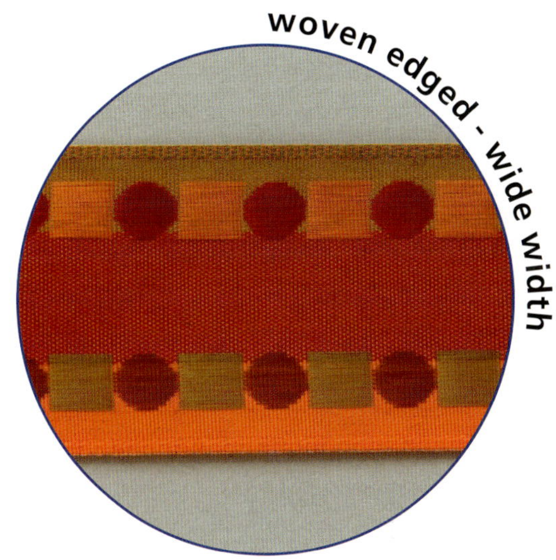

3 WOVEN EDGED RIBBONS WITH WIRE

If you found the perfect ribbon for a project but it has a wired edge, you can still use it. The ribbon used in the Blanket is this type of ribbon. You simply pull the wire from the edges.

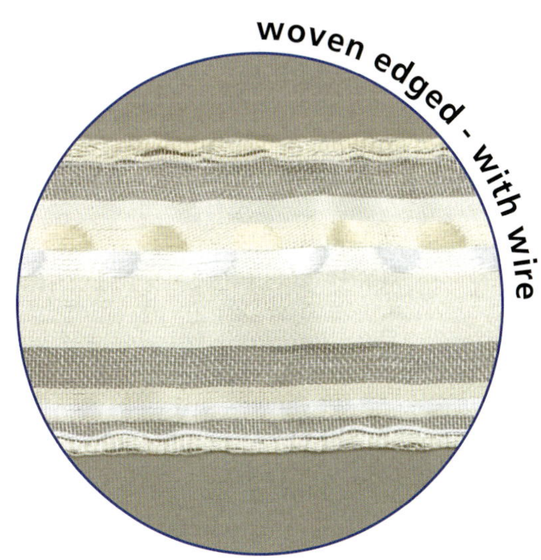

4 UNSUITABLE RIBBONS

Cut edged ribbon which is made from fabric that has been slit into ribbon widths and treated with a stiffening agent is not suitable for these projects.

Buying RIBBON

Ribbon yarn is made by many manufacturers and can be found at most stores that carry yarn. You can also buy ribbon yarn on the internet through suppliers for the yarn companies.

Woven ribbon can be found in most fabric or craft stores and also on the internet.

Refer to the Yarn Information, page 48, for a list of ribbons used to create our photography models.

Washing & *Care*

Ribbon can be made from 100% nylon and/or blends including polyester, rayon, and acrylic. Be sure to check the label for fiber content and washing instructions. Most of the ribbons we used need to be hand washed and allowed to air dry.

WORKING WITH *Balls* OF RIBBON

Place a rubber band around the ball of ribbon to keep the outer layers from falling off the ball. You may need to occasionally un-twist the ball.

Joining RIBBON

Begin working into ribbon, leaving a length long enough to be secured to work later.

To join ribbon to your crochet, it is often necessary to change hook sizes in the middle of a row or round so that the hook will be small enough to fit through the ribbon.

Transfer the loop from one hook to the other as needed.

Ribbon TECHNIQUES

MAKING *Holes* IN THE RIBBON

If the ribbon you are using is tightly woven, you may need to make holes in it first in order to make it easy to insert the crochet hook. Do this just before you are ready to crochet into it, so the holes won't close and disappear.

With a permanent marker, mark a tapestry needle 1" (2.5 cm) and $1^1/_2$" (4 cm) from the point for a placement guide.

If the holes in the ribbon need to be 1" (2.5 cm) apart, insert the needle in the edge of the ribbon up to the first mark; if they need to be $1^1/_2$" (4 cm), insert the needle in the edge of the ribbon up to the second mark. Holding the ribbon close to the mark and using the marked length as a guide ***(Fig. 1a)***, continue inserting the needle in the ribbon, alternating from front to back ***(Fig. 1b)***.

Fig. 1a

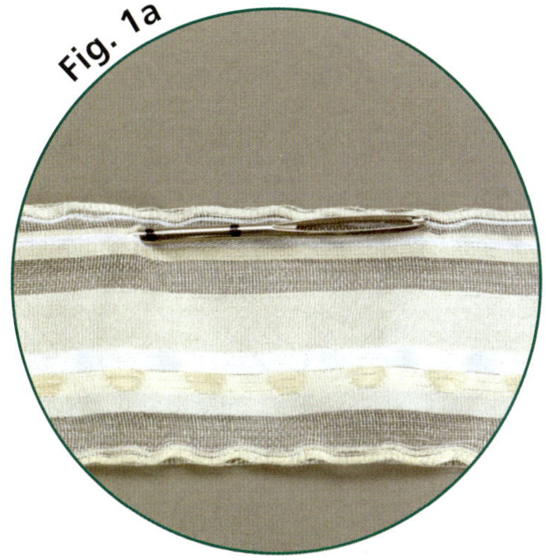

Fig. 1b

Working INTO RIBBON

Flowers and ruffles can be added anywhere you want on your project. There are two ways to do this. Either add the flowers or ruffles as you crochet the body of your piece, or add them as part of the finished edge.

When adding Ruffles, begin by leaving a long length of ribbon that will be tacked to the wrong side.

To begin a chain of flowers, start with a slip knot on the hook, then chain one. You are ready to make the first flower.

Whether you're making a ribbon flower or joining the ribbon to your crocheted piece, it's easy to achieve uniform petals and ruffles. Measure the hook from the tip to 1¾" (4.5 cm). It will be near the center of the finger hold ***(Fig. 2a)***.

To insert the hook through the ribbon at the same distance without measuring each time, push the loop on the hook to the same approximate place and insert the hook through the ribbon at this length, either at the center of ribbon or at the edge ***(Fig. 2b)*** as specified in individual instructions.

Fig. 2a

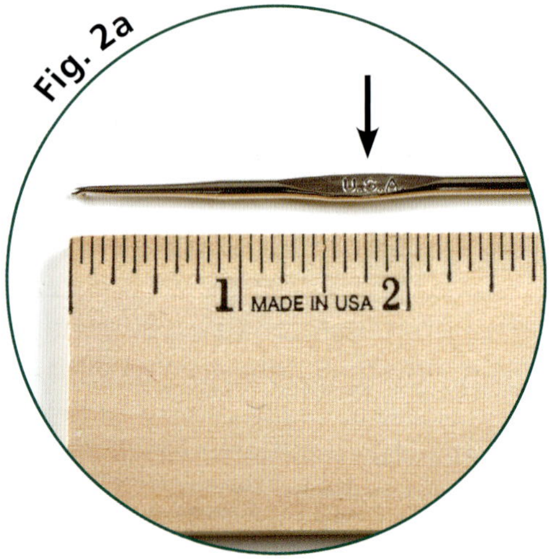

Fig. 2b

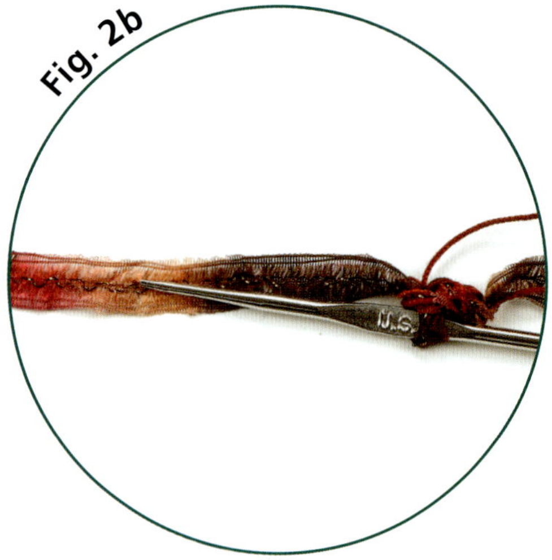

ALL ABOUT RIBBON *Flowers*

Flowers can be different sizes depending on the width of the ribbon used and on how many loops are formed. We used the following two styles to make the flowers for our projects.

1 THE BOW LOOPS STYLE

Petals: Using smaller size hook, insert hook through ribbon and push ribbon next to loop on hook ***(Fig. 3a)***, ★ insert hook back into same side of ribbon as you last came out of and push ribbon next to loop on hook; repeat from ★ as many times **more** as specified in individual instructions ***(Fig. 3b)***, with thread, and keeping the loops from turning around the hook, YO and carefully draw through all ribbon holes leaving previous loop on hook ***(Fig. 3c)***:
2 loops on hook.

Repeat Petals the number of times specified in individual instructions.

With thread, YO and draw through all loops on hook ***(Fig. 3d)***.

Fig. 3a

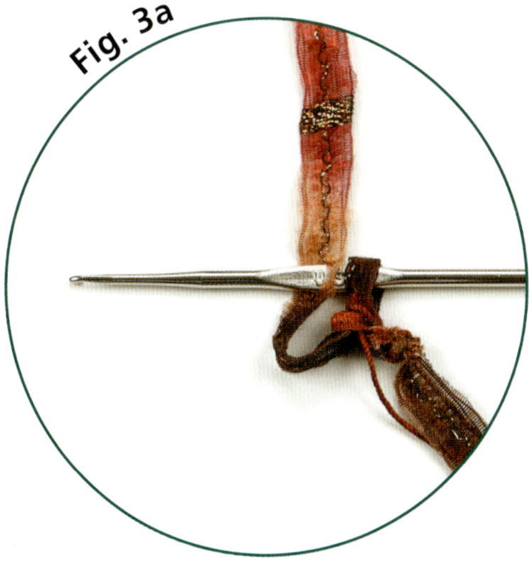

Fig. 3b

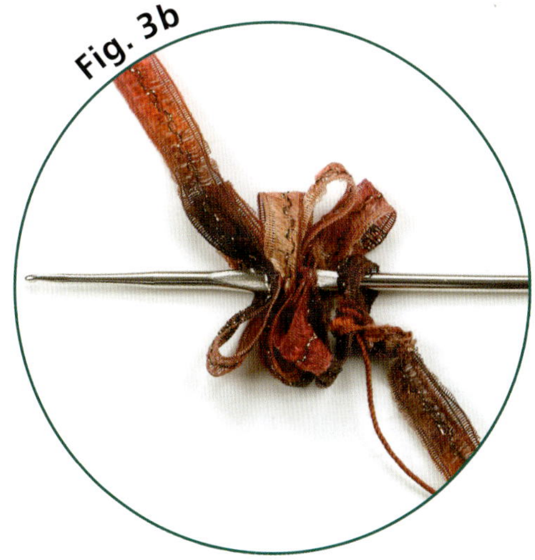

Fig. 3c

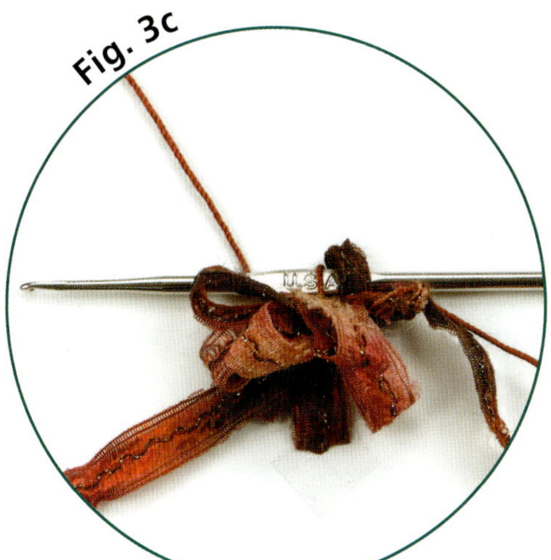

Fig. 3d

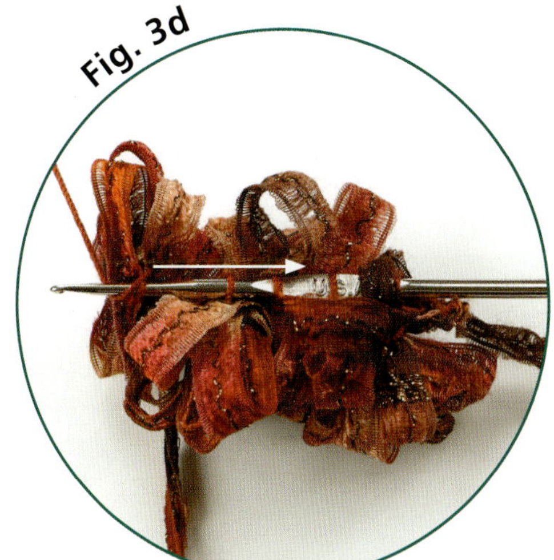

2 THE GATHERED (CLUSTER) STYLE

When using ribbon with holes, the instructions will indicate how many holes to skip before inserting the hook into the ribbon. When using solid ribbon, insert the hook about 1¾" (4.5 cm) from the tip of the hook.

Petals: ★ Insert hook through ribbon and slide previous loop on hook next to ribbon at tip of hook ***(Fig. 4a)***, with thread or yarn, YO and pull up a loop through ribbon ***(Fig. 4b)***; repeat from ★ as many times **more** as specified in individual instructions keeping loops on hook close together ***(Fig. 4c)***, YO and draw through all thread or yarn loops just formed. You will have one thread or yarn loop and one combination loop on hook ***(Fig. 4d)***.

Repeat Petals the number of times specified in individual instructions. You will have one thread or yarn loop for each group of petals made and one combination loop on hook.

With thread or yarn, YO and draw through all loops on hook, ch 1 to close ***(Fig. 4e)***.

Fig. 4a

Fig. 4b

Fig. 4c

Fig. 4d

Fig. 4e

ALL ABOUT RIBBON *Ruffles*

To add ribbon ruffles, you can join ribbon to your crocheted piece in one of two ways. Either pull a loop of yarn through the ribbon or insert the hook through the ribbon as you finish a stitch.

1 JOINING RIBBON WITH LOOP

Drop loop from hook, insert smaller size hook through the edge of the ribbon, spacing holes as specified in individual instructions ***(Fig. 5a)***, and pull the dropped loop through the ribbon. Change back to larger size hook ***(Fig. 5b)***.

Fig. 5a

Fig. 5b

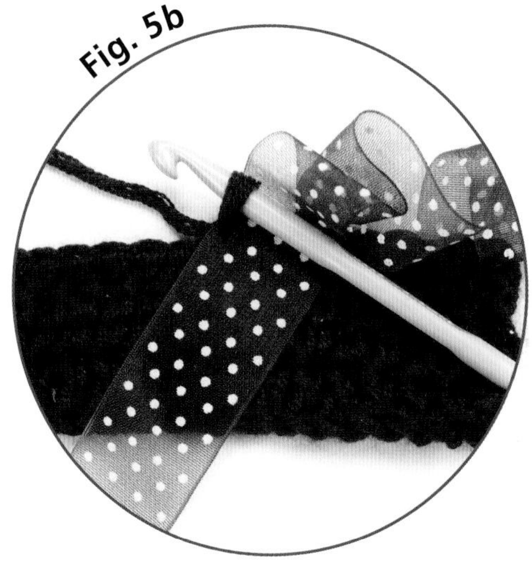

2 JOINING RIBBON WITH A STITCH

Joining ribbon in front: Begin working a slip st, sc or dc, first inserting the hook through the ribbon ***(Fig. 6a)***, then in the next stitch ***(Fig. 6b)*** and complete the stitch ***(Fig. 6c)***.

Joining ribbon in back: Begin working a slip st, sc or dc, first inserting the hook in the next stitch, then through the ribbon ***(Fig. 6d)*** and complete the stitch ***(Fig. 6e)***.

Fig. 6a

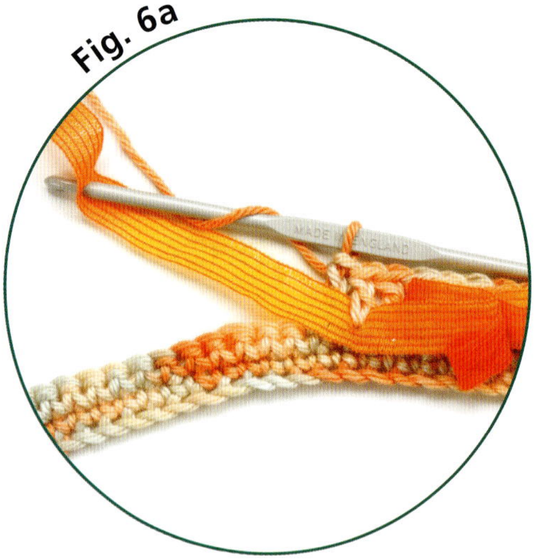

Fig. 6b

Fig. 6c

Fig. 6d

Fig. 6e

Necklace

BEGINNER

Finished Length: 20" (51 cm)

MATERIALS

BULKY 5

- Bulky Weight Ribbon Yarn (solid style) **[**1.75 ounces, 110 yards (50 grams, 100 meters) per ball**]**:1 ball
- 100% Cotton Thread, size 5 **[**191 yards (175 meters) per ball**]**:1 ball
- Steel crochet hook, size 2 (2.25 mm)
- E-Beads size 6/0 - 196
- Tapestry needle (small enough to fit through your beads)

RIBBON FLOWER

To insert the hook through the ribbon at the same distance without measuring each time, push the loop on the hook about $1\frac{3}{4}$" (4.5 cm) from the tip (near the center of the finger hold). Using this as a guide, insert the hook through the center of the ribbon at this length ***(Figs. 2a & b, page 6)***.

Petals: ★ With loop on hook $1\frac{3}{4}$" (4.5 cm) from tip, insert hook through ribbon and slide previous loop on hook next to ribbon at tip of hook, with thread YO and pull up a loop through ribbon; repeat from ★ 5 times **more** keeping loops on hook close together, YO and draw through 6 thread loops. Repeat Petals 2 times **more**: 3 thread loops and one combination loop. With thread, YO and draw through all loops on hook, ch 1 to close ***(Figs. 4a-e, page 8)***.

NECKLACE

Thread tapestry needle with thread still attached to the ball and string all beads onto the thread ***(Fig. 12, page 47)***. Push beads down close to the ball until they are needed.

Holding ribbon and thread together ch 1, ★ make Ribbon Flower; holding ribbon and thread together ch 1; drop thread, with ribbon ch 6, push 14 beads up close to work ***(Fig. 7a)***; holding ribbon and thread together ch 1 ***(Fig. 7b)***; repeat from ★ 13 times **more**; join with slip st to first ch, finish off.✻

Fig. 7a

Fig. 7b

Hat

EASY

Finished Size: 20" (51 cm) head circumference

MATERIALS

Light Weight Yarn (LIGHT 3)
[2.5 ounces, 168 yards (70 grams, 154 meters) per skein]:1 skein
Bulky Weight Ribbon Yarn (railroad or lacy ladder style) (BULKY 5)
[1.75 ounces, 92 yards (50 grams, 84 meters) per ball]:1 ball
100% Cotton Thread, size 5
[191 yards (175 meters) per ball]:1 ball
Crochet hook, size H (5 mm) **or** size needed for gauge
Steel crochet hook, size 6 (1.8 mm)

GAUGE: With larger size hook and light weight yarn, in pattern, (3 dc, ch 4) 3 times = 3¾" (9.5 cm); 9 rows = 4" (10 cm)

Gauge Swatch: 3¾" (9.5 cm) diameter
Work same as Body through Rnd 4.

RIBBON FLOWER

To insert the hook through the ribbon at the same distance without measuring each time, push the loop on the hook about 1¾" (4.5 cm) from the tip (near the center of the finger hold). Using this as a guide, insert the hook through the center of the ribbon at this length ***(Figs. 2a & b, page 6)***.

Petals: Using smaller size hook ***(see Joining Ribbon and Changing Hook Size, page 4)***, insert hook through ribbon and push ribbon next to loop on hook, ★ insert hook back into same side of ribbon as you last came out of and push ribbon next to loop on hook; repeat from ★ 8 times **more**, with thread YO and draw through all ribbon holes leaving previous loop on hook: 2 loops on hook. Repeat Petals,2 times **more**: 4 loops on hook. With thread, YO and draw through all 4 loops on hook ***(Figs. 3a-d, page 7)***.

BODY

With larger size hook and light weight yarn, ch 6; join with slip st to form a ring.

Rnd 1 (Right side)**:** Ch 5, (dc in ring, ch 2) 7 times; join with slip st to third ch of beginning ch-5: 8 sps.

Rnd 2: Slip st in first sp, ch 8, (dc in next ch-2 sp, ch 5) around; join with slip st to third ch of beginning ch-8.

Rnd 3: Ch 1, sc in same st as joining, ch 4, sc in next ch-5 sp, ch 4, ★ sc in next dc, ch 4, sc in next ch-5 sp, ch 4; repeat from ★ around; join with slip st to first sc: 16 ch-4 sps.

Rnd 4: Slip st in first ch-4 sp, ch 3 **(counts as first dc, now and throughout)**, 2 dc in same sp, 3 dc in next ch-4 sp and in each ch-4 sp around; join with slip st to first dc: 48 dc.

Rnd 5: Ch 3, dc in next dc and in each dc around; join with slip st to first dc.

Rnds 6 and 7: Ch 3, dc in next 2 dc, ch 1, (dc in next 3 dc, ch 1) around; join with slip st to first dc: 48 dc and 16 ch-1 sps.

Rnds 8-11: Ch 3, dc in next 2 dc, ch 2, (dc in next 3 dc, ch 2) around; join with slip st to first dc.

Rnds 12-14: Ch 3, dc in next 2 dc, ch 3, (dc in next 3 dc, ch 3) around; join with slip st to first dc.

Rnds 15-19: Ch 3, dc in next 2 dc, ch 4, (dc in next 3 dc, ch 4) around; join with slip st to first dc.

Finish off.

FLOWER EDGING

With larger size hook and holding one strand each of ribbon and thread together, join with slip st in first ch-4 sp; ch 1, 2 sc in same sp, sc in next dc, change to smaller size hook and make Ribbon Flower, ★ change to larger size hook and holding ribbon and thread together, 2 sc in next ch-4 sp, sc in next dc, change to smaller size hook and make Ribbon Flower; repeat from ★ around; change to larger size hook and holding ribbon and thread together, join with slip st to first sc, finish off.

Scarf

BEGINNER

Finished Size: 5 1/2" x 66" (14 cm x 167.5 cm)

MATERIALS

Bulky Weight Ribbon Yarn (solid style) BULKY 5
[1.76 ounces, 93 yards
(50 grams, 85 meters) per ball]: 2 balls
100% Cotton Thread, size 5
[191 yards (175 meters) per ball]:1 ball
Crochet hook, size H (5 mm) **or** size needed for gauge
Steel crochet hook, size 6 (1.8 mm)

GAUGE: One Ribbon Flower and
12 chs = 3 1/2" (9 cm)

Gauge Swatch: 7" (17.75 cm)
With larger size hook and holding ribbon and thread together, ch 2, ★ change to smaller size hook and make Ribbon Flower, change to larger size hook and holding ribbon and thread together, ch 12; repeat from ★ once **more**.

RIBBON FLOWER

To insert the hook through the ribbon at the same distance without measuring each time, push the loop on the hook about 1 3/4" (4.5 cm) from the tip (near the center of the finger hold). Using this as a guide, insert the hook through the center of the ribbon at this length ***(Figs. 2a & b, page 6)***.

Petals: Using smaller size hook ***(see Joining Ribbon and Changing Hook Size, page 4)***, insert hook through ribbon and push ribbon next to loop on hook, ★ insert hook back into same side of ribbon as you last came out of and push ribbon next to loop on hook; repeat from ★ 6 times **more**, with thread YO, and draw through all ribbon holes leaving previous loop on hook: 2 loops on hook. Repeat Petals, 4 times **more**: 6 loops on hook. With thread, YO and draw through all 6 loops on hook ***(Figs. 3a-d, page 7)***.

PLACEMENT DIAGRAM

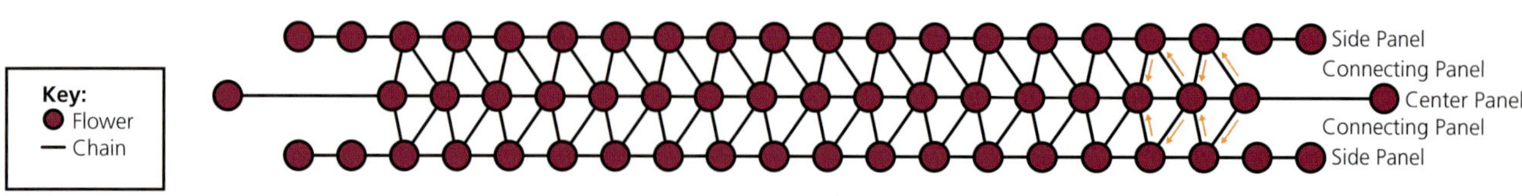

SIDE PANELS (Make 2)

With larger size hook and holding ribbon and thread together, ch 2, change to smaller size hook and make Ribbon Flower, ★ change to larger size hook and holding ribbon and thread together, ch 12, change to smaller size hook and make Ribbon Flower; repeat from ★ 18 times **more**; finish off: 20 Flowers.

CENTER PANEL

With larger size hook and holding ribbon and thread together, ch 2, change to smaller size hook and make Ribbon Flower, change to larger size hook and holding ribbon and thread together, ch 25, change to smaller size hook and make Ribbon Flower, ★ change to larger size hook and holding ribbon and thread together, ch 12, change to smaller size hook and make Ribbon Flower; repeat from ★ 15 times **more**, change to larger size hook and holding ribbon and thread together, ch 25, change to smaller size hook and make Ribbon Flower; finish off: 19 Flowers.

CONNECTING PANELS

Refer to diagram, page 14, for joining placement. With larger size hook, holding ribbon and thread together, and working in back of Ribbon Flowers, join with slip st in second Flower on Center Panel, ch 12, slip st in third Flower on Side Panel, ch 12, slip st in next Flower on Center Panel, ★ ch 12, slip st in next Flower on Side Panel, ch 12, slip st in next Flower on Center Panel; repeat from ★ 14 times **more**; finish off.

Connect second Side Panel in same manner.*

Pillow

EASY

Finished Size: 18" (45.5 cm) square

MATERIALS

100% Cotton Light Weight Yarn (LIGHT 3)
[1.75 ounces, 136 yards
(50 grams, 125 meters) per skein]:
4 skeins
Bulky Weight Ribbon Yarn (BULKY 5)
(solid style) [1.75 ounces, 80 yards
(50 grams, 73 meters) per ball]:
1 ball
Crochet hook, size G (4 mm) **or** size
needed for gauge
18" (45.5 cm) Pillow form

GAUGE: With light weight yarn,
19 dc and 9 rows = 4"
(10 cm)

Gauge Swatch: 4" (10 cm) square
With light weight yarn, ch 21.
Rows 1-9: Work same as Back.
Finish off.

JOINING RIBBON WITH DC

To insert the hook through the ribbon at the same distance without measuring each time, push the loop on the hook about 1¾" (4.5 cm) from the tip (near the center of the finger hold). Using this as a guide, insert the hook through the center of the ribbon at this length ***(Figs. 2a & b page 6)***.

Joining ribbon in front: YO, insert hook through ribbon, then in next dc and complete dc ***(Figs. 6a-c, page 10)***.

Joining ribbon in back: YO, insert hook in next dc then through ribbon, and complete dc ***(Figs. 6d & e, page 10)***.

BACK

With light weight yarn, ch 86.

Row 1 (Right side)**:** Dc in fourth ch from hook **(3 skipped chs count as first dc, now and throughout)** and in each ch across: 84 dc.

Note: Loop a short piece of yarn around any stitch to mark Row 1 as **right** side.

Rows 2-45: Ch 3 **(counts as first dc, now and throughout)**, turn; dc in next dc and in each dc across.

Finish off.

FRONT

With light weight yarn, ch 86.

Row 1 (Right side)**:** Dc in fourth ch from hook and in each ch across: 84 dc.

Note: Mark Row 1 as **right** side.

Rows 2-8: Ch 3, turn; dc in next dc and in each dc across.

When you join ribbon for the first time on Row 9, leave a long length that will be tacked to the wrong side. Do not cut ribbon at end of rows; allow ribbon to hang on the right side and form a loose loop when beginning next ribbon row.

Row 9 (Joining ribbon)**:** Ch 3, turn; dc in next dc, dc in next dc joining ribbon in **front**, (dc in next 3 dc, dc in next dc joining ribbon in **front**) across to last dc, dc in last dc: 20 ribbon loops.

Row 10 (Joining ribbon)**:** Ch 3, turn; dc in next 2 dc, dc in next dc joining ribbon in **back**, (dc in next 3 dc, dc in next dc joining ribbon in **back**) across to last 4 dc, dc in next 2 dc, dc in next dc joining ribbon in **back**, dc in last dc: 21 ribbon loops.

Rows 11 and 12: Ch 3, turn; dc in next dc and in each dc across.

Rows 13-15: Repeat Rows 9 and 10 once, then repeat Row 9 once **more**.

Rows 16 and 17: Ch 3, turn; dc in next dc and in each dc across.

Rows 18-22: Repeat Row 10, then repeat Rows 9 and 10 twice.

Rows 23 and 24: Ch 3, turn; dc in next dc and in each dc across.

Rows 25-29: Repeat Rows 9 and 10 twice, then repeat Row 9 once **more**.

Rows 30 and 31: Ch 3, turn; dc in next dc and in each dc across.

Rows 32-34: Repeat Row 10, then repeat Rows 9 and 10 once.

Rows 35 and 36: Ch 3, turn; dc in next dc and in each dc across.

Rows 37 and 38: Repeat Rows 9 and 10.

Cut ribbon leaving a length that will be tacked to wrong side.

Rows 39-45: Ch 3, turn; dc in next dc and in each dc across.

Finish off.

Weave in yarn ends. Tack ribbon ends to **wrong** side.

With **wrong** sides together, whipstitch Front and Back together across 3 sides ***(Fig. 11a, page 47)***; insert pillow form and whipstitch remaining side.✻

Purse

EASY

Finished Size: 9½" high x 13" wide at bottom (24 cm x 33 cm)

MATERIALS

MEDIUM 4

Medium Weight Yarn
[5 ounces, 256 yards
(140 grams, 234 meters) per skein]:1 skein
1 7/16" (36 mm) wide Woven Ribbon (large dot)
[10 yards (9.5 meters) per spool]: 1 spool
Crochet hooks, sizes B (2 mm) **and** H (5 mm)
or sizes needed for gauge
Yarn needle
* Exclusively You 13" (33 cm) smooth double purse handles - #28304 Green

GAUGE: With larger size hook and medium weight yarn, 17 dc and 9 rows = 4" (10 cm)

Gauge Swatch: 4" (10 cm) square
With larger size hook and medium weight yarn, ch 19.
Row 1: Dc in fourth ch from hook **(3 skipped chs count as first dc)** and in each ch across: 17 dc.
Rows 2-9: Ch 3 **(counts as first dc)**, turn; dc in next dc and in each dc across.
Finish off.

* If you are unable to find Exclusively You handles at your local retailer visit TheLeisureBoutique.com for the entire product line.

STITCH GUIDE

DECREASE (uses next 2 dc)
★ YO, insert hook in **next** dc, YO and pull up a loop, YO and draw through 2 loops on hook; repeat from ★ once **more**, YO and draw through all 3 loops on hook **(counts as one dc)**.

JOINING RIBBON WITH LOOP

Drop loop from hook, insert smaller size hook through the edge of the ribbon spacing holes about 2¼" (5.5 cm) apart (over the fourth dot) and pull the dropped loop through the ribbon ***(Figs. 5a & b, page 9)***. Change back to larger size hook.

Instructions continued on page 20.

BODY

With larger size hook and yarn, ch 112; join with slip st to form a ring being careful not to twist ch.

Rnd 1 (Right side)**:** Ch 1, sc in same st as joining and in each ch around; join with slip st to first sc: 112 sc.

Note: Loop a short piece of yarn around any stitch to mark Rnd 1 as **right** side.

Rnds 2 and 3: Ch 1, do **not** turn; sc in same st as joining and in each sc around; join with slip st to first sc.

Rnd 4 (Increase row)**:** Ch 1, sc in same st as joining and in next 12 sc, 2 sc in next sc, (sc in next 13 sc, 2 sc in next sc) around; join with slip st to first sc: 120 sc.

When you join ribbon for the first time on Rnd 5, leave a long length that will be tacked to the wrong side. Do not cut ribbon at end of rounds; allow ribbon to hang on the right side and form a loose loop when beginning next ribbon round.

Rnd 5 (Joining ribbon)**:** Ch 3 **(counts as first dc, now and throughout)**, dc in next 3 sts, join ribbon with loop, (dc in next 4 sts, join ribbon with loop) around; join with slip st to first dc.

Rnd 6: Ch 3, dc in next dc and in each dc around; join with slip st to first dc.

Rnd 7: Ch 3, dc in next 7 dc, decrease, (dc in next 8 dc, decrease) around; join with slip st to first dc: 108 dc.

Rnds 8 and 9: Repeat Rnds 5 and 6.

Rnd 10: Ch 3, dc in next 6 dc, decrease, (dc in next 7 dc, decrease) around; join with slip st to first dc: 96 dc.

Rnds 11 and 12: Repeat Rnds 5 and 6.

Rnd 13: Ch 3, dc in next 5 dc, decrease, (dc in next 6 dc, decrease) around; join with slip st to first dc: 84 dc.

Rnds 14 and 15: Repeat Rnds 5 and 6.

Rnd 16: Ch 3, dc in next 4 dc, decrease, (dc in next 5 dc, decrease) around; join with slip st to first dc: 72 dc.

Rnds 17 and 18: Repeat Rnds 5 and 6.

Rnd 19: Ch 3, dc in next 6 dc, decrease, (dc in next 7 dc, decrease) around; join with slip st to first dc: 64 dc.

Rnd 20 (Joining ribbon)**:** Ch 1, join ribbon with loop 2¼" (5.5 cm) from last joining, sc in first 2 dc, **[**join ribbon with loop 1¼" (3 cm) from last joining, sc in next 2 dc**]** around; join with slip st to first sc.

Cut ribbon leaving a length that will be tacked to wrong side.

Rnds 21-28: Ch 1, sc in each sc around; join with slip st to first sc.

Finish off.

With **right** sides together and placing joining at center back, sew bottom seam.

With yarn, sew purse handles to purse at sides.

Weave in yarn ends. Tack ribbon ends on inside of purse.

Blanket

Shown on page 23.

EASY

Finished Size: 37" (94 cm) square

MATERIALS

Medium Weight Yarn (MEDIUM 4)
[6 ounces, 315 yards
(170 grams, 288 meters) per skein]:5 skeins
$1^1/_2$" (38.1 mm) wide Woven Ribbon
[4 yards (3.65 meters) per spool]: 3 spools
Crochet hooks, sizes E (3.5 mm) **and** H (5 mm)
or sizes needed for gauge
Tapestry needle

GAUGE SWATCH: $3^3/_4$" (9.5 cm) square
Work same as Square.

STITCH GUIDE

BEGINNING CLUSTER (uses one sp)
Ch 3, ★ YO, insert hook in ring, YO and pull up a loop, YO and draw through 2 loops on hook; repeat from ★ 3 times **more**, YO and draw through all 5 loops on hook.
CLUSTER (uses one sp)
★ YO, insert hook in ring, YO and pull up a loop, YO and draw through 2 loops on hook; repeat from ★ 4 times **more**, YO and draw through all 6 loops on hook.

JOINING RIBBON WITH SC

Hold ribbon behind blanket with **wrong** sides together and edges even with top of Rnd 2. Change to smaller size hook ***(see Joining Ribbon and Changing Hook Size, page 4)***, and insert hook in next ch-3 sp then through hole made in ribbon, YO and pull up a loop, change to larger size hook, complete sc ***(Figs. 6a-c, page 10)***.

JOINING RIBBON WITH SLIP STITCH

Using smaller size hook, insert hook in next st then through hole made in ribbon from back to front, YO and pull loop through ribbon and all loops on hook.

SQUARE (Make 81)

With larger size hook and yarn, ch 7; join with slip st to form a ring.

Rnd 1: Work beginning Cluster in ring, ch 5, (work Cluster in ring, ch 5) 3 times; join with slip st to top of beginning Cluster: 4 ch-5 sps.

Rnd 2 (Right side)**:** Turn; slip st in first ch-5 sp, ch 3 **(counts as first dc, now and throughout)**, (2 dc, ch 3, 3 dc) in same sp, ch 2, ★ (3 dc, ch 3, 3 dc) in next ch-5 sp, ch 2; repeat from ★ around; join with slip st to first dc: 24 dc and 8 sps.

Note: Loop a short piece of yarn around any stitch to mark Rnd 2 as **right** side.

Instructions continued on page 22.

Rnd 3: Do **not** turn; slip st in next 2 dc and in next ch, ch 1, sc in same ch-3 sp, ch 2, (3 dc, ch 3, 3 dc) in next ch-2 sp, ch 2, ★ sc in next ch-3 sp, ch 2, (3 dc, ch 3, 3 dc) in next ch-2 sp, ch 2; repeat from ★ around; join with slip st to first sc: 24 dc and 4 sc.

Rnd 4: Ch 3, (3 dc, ch 3, 4 dc) in same st as joining, ch 3, skip next ch-2 sp, sc in next ch-3 sp, ch 3, ★ (4 dc, ch 3) twice in next sc, skip next ch-2 sp, sc in next ch-3 sp, ch 3; repeat from ★ around; join with slip st to first dc, finish off: 32 dc and 4 sc.

ASSEMBLY

With **wrong** sides together and working through **inside** loops only, whipstitch Squares together forming 9 vertical strips of 9 Squares each *(Fig. 11b, page 47)*, beginning in center ch of first corner ch-3 and ending in center ch of next corner ch-3; then whipstitch strips together in same manner.

OUTSIDE EDGING

Rnd 1: With **right** side facing and larger size hook, join yarn with slip st in any corner ch-3 sp; ch 3, 4 dc in same sp, working in Back Loops Only *(Fig. 9, page 47)*, work 15 dc evenly spaced across each Square to next corner ch-3 sp, ★ 5 dc in corner ch-3 sp, work 15 dc evenly spaced across each Square to next corner ch-3 sp; repeat from ★ around; join with slip st to first dc: 560 dc.

Rnd 2: Ch 6, dc in same st as joining, ch 3, skip next 3 dc, dc in next dc, ch 3, skip next 3 dc, ★ (dc, ch 3) twice in next dc, skip next 3 dc, dc in next dc, ch 3, skip next 3 dc; repeat from ★ around; join with slip st to third ch of beginning ch-6: 210 sts and 210 ch-3 sps.

Prepare Ribbon making holes 1½" (4 cm) apart *(Figs. 1a-c, page 5)*.

Rnd 3 (Joining ribbon)**:** Slip st in first ch-3 sp, ch 3, (3 dc, ch 3, 4 dc) in same sp, join ribbon with sc in next ch-3 sp, ch 3, join ribbon with sc in next ch-3 sp, ★ (4 dc, ch 3, 4 dc) in next ch-3 sp, join ribbon with sc in next ch-3 sp, ch 3, join ribbon with sc in next ch-3 sp; repeat from ★ around working through 2 ribbon holes before and after each corner; join with slip st to first dc, finish off.

INSIDE EDGING

Prepare Ribbon making holes 1" (2.5 cm) apart.

With **right** side facing, using smaller size hook, and working in free loops of sts across 5 Squares on each side as indicated on Placement Diagram, join yarn with slip st in corner st; (loosely slip st in next st, join ribbon with slip st in next st) around also working in joinings; join with slip st to first st, finish off.

Weave in yarn ends. Sew ends of ribbon together on both Edgings.

PLACEMENT DIAGRAM

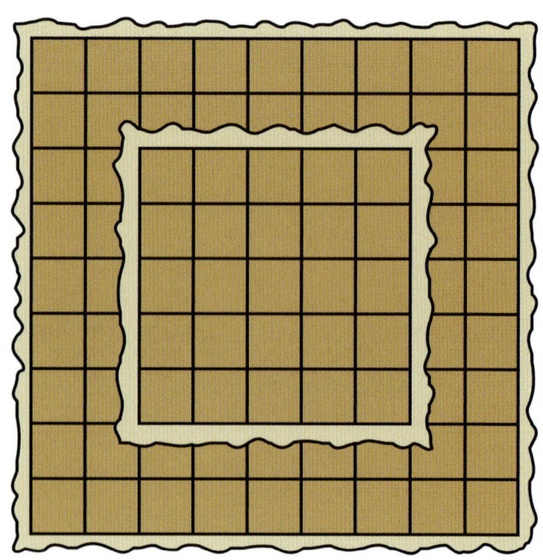

Triangular Shawl

BEGINNER

Finished Size: 54" (137 cm) across top edge

MATERIALS

SUPER BULKY 6

Super Bulky Weight Ribbon Yarn (checkerboard style)
[1.76 ounces, 28 yards (50 grams, 26 meters) per ball]: 8 balls
100% Cotton Thread, size 5
[191 yards (175 meters) per ball]:1 ball
Crochet hooks, sizes D (3.25 mm) **and** I (5.5 mm) **or** sizes needed for gauge

GAUGE: With larger size hook, One Ribbon Flower and 10 chs = 3½" (9 cm)

Gauge Swatch: 7" (17.75 cm)
With larger size hook and holding ribbon and thread together, ch 1, ★ change to smaller size hook and make Ribbon Flower, change to larger size hook and holding ribbon and thread together, ch 10; repeat from ★ once **more**.

RIBBON FLOWER

Petals: Using smaller size hook ***(see Joining Ribbon and Changing Hook Size, page 4)*** and working in second row of holes, skip 5 squares from loop on hook and insert hook through next hole on ribbon and slide previous loop on hook next to ribbon at tip of hook, with thread, YO and pull up a loop through ribbon, ★ skip 4 squares from loop on hook and insert hook through next hole on ribbon and slide loop on hook next to ribbon at tip of hook, with thread, YO and pull up a loop through ribbon; repeat from ★ 4 times **more** keeping loops on hook close together, YO and draw through 6 thread loops: one thread loop and one combination loop. Repeat Petals 3 times **more**: 4 thread loops and one combination loop. With thread, YO and draw through all loops on hook, ch 1 to close ***(Figs. 4a-e, page 8)***,

.

STRIPS

TOP STRIP

With larger size hook and holding ribbon and thread together, ch 1, change to smaller size hook and make Ribbon Flower, ★ change to larger size hook and holding ribbon and thread together, ch 10, change to smaller size hook and make Ribbon Flower; repeat from ★ 14 times **more**; finish off: 16 Flowers.

REMAINING 14 STRIPS

Work same as Top Strip working one less Flower for each Strip. Last Strip will have 2 Flowers.

FLOWER FOR POINT

With larger size hook and holding ribbon and thread together, ch 1, change to smaller size hook and make Ribbon Flower; finish off.

JOINING STRIPS

With larger size hook and working in back of Ribbon Flowers, join ribbon with slip st in first Flower on Top Strip, ch 6, slip st in first Flower on second Strip (with 15 Flowers), ★ ch 6, slip st in next Flower on previous Strip; repeat from ★ across, ending on longer Strip; finish off.

Connect each Strip to previous Strip in same manner.

JOINING POINT

With larger size hook and ribbon and working in back of Ribbon Flowers, join ribbon with slip st in first Flower on last Strip, ch 6, slip st in Flower for point, ch 6, slip st in next Flower on previous Strip; finish off.

Weave in ends.✻

Bolero

INTERMEDIATE

Size	Finished Length (Cuff to Cuff)	
Small	52"	(132 cm)
Medium	55"	(139.5 cm)
Large	58"	(147.5 cm)

Size Note: Instructions are written for size Small with sizes Medium and Large in braces { }. Instructions will be easier to read if you circle all the numbers pertaining to your size. If only one number is given, it applies to all sizes.

MATERIALS

Light Weight Yarn (LIGHT 3)
[2.5 ounces, 168 yards (70 grams, 154 meters) per skein]: 5{6-6} skeins
7/8" (22 mm) wide Woven Ribbon (small dot) [7 yards (6.4 meters) per spool]: 2 spools
Crochet hook, size H (5 mm) **or** size needed for gauge
Steel crochet hook, size 6 (1.8 mm)

GAUGE: With larger size hook and light weight yarn, in pattern, 4 Shells and 8 rows = 4" (10 cm)

Gauge Swatch: 4 3/4"w x 4 1/4"h (12 cm x 10.75 cm)
With larger size hook and yarn, ch 18.
Row 1: Sc in second ch from hook and in each ch across: 17 sc.
Row 2: Ch 4 **(counts as first dc plus ch 1, now and throughout)**, turn; 3 dc in first sc **(counts as first Shell)**, (skip next 3 sc, work Shell in next sc) 3 times, skip next 3 sc, (dc, ch 1, dc) in last sc: 4 Shells and 1 ch-1 sp.
Rows 3-9: Work beginning Shell, work Shell in each Shell (ch-1 sp) across to last Shell, (dc, ch 1, dc) in last Shell.
Finish off.

STITCH GUIDE

BEGINNING SHELL
Ch 4, turn; 3 dc in first ch-1 sp.
SHELL
(Dc, ch 1, 3 dc) in st or sp indicated.
SC DECREASE
Pull up a loop in each of next 2 sts, YO and draw through all 3 loops on hook **(counts as one sc)**.

JOINING RIBBON WITH LOOP

Drop loop from hook, insert smaller size hook through the edge of the ribbon spacing holes about 2 1/4" (5.5 cm) apart (over the sixth dot) and pull the loop through the ribbon ***(Figs. 5a & b, page 9)***. Change back to larger size hook.

Instructions begin on page 28.

This Bolero is worked from Cuff to Cuff.

RIGHT SLEEVE

With larger size hook and yarn, ch 42{46-50} **loosely**.

Row 1: Sc in second ch from hook and in each ch across: 41{45-49} sc.

Row 2: Ch 1, turn; sc in each sc across.

Row 3: Ch 4 **(counts as first dc plus ch 1, now and throughout)**, turn; 3 dc in first sc **(counts as first Shell)**, (skip next 3 sc, work Shell in next sc) 9{10-11} times, skip next 3 sc, (dc, ch 1, dc) in last sc: 10{11-12} Shells and one ch-1 sp.

Rows 4 thru 8{9-10}: Work beginning Shell, work Shell in each Shell (ch-1 sp) across to last Shell, (dc, ch 1, dc) in last Shell; do **not** finish off.

SHAPING

Row 1 (Right side)**:** Work beginning Shell, work Shell in each Shell across: 11{12-13} Shells.

Note: Loop a short piece of yarn around any stitch to mark Row 1 as **right** side.

Row 2: Ch 4, turn; work Shell in first Shell and in each Shell across: 11{12-13} Shells and one ch-1 sp.

Row 3: Ch 4, turn; work Shell in first Shell and in each Shell across, (dc, ch 1, dc) in last ch-1 sp: 11{12-13} Shells and 2 ch-1 sps.

Row 4: Work beginning Shell, work Shell in each Shell across, (dc, ch 1, dc) in last ch-1 sp: 12{13-14} Shells and one ch-1 sp.

Rows 5-28: Repeat Rows 1-4, 6 times; do **not** finish off: 24{25-26} Shells and one ch-1 sp.

BACK

Row 1: Work beginning Shell, work Shell in next 9{10-11} Shells, (dc, ch 1, dc) in next Shell; leave remaining 14 Shells unworked: 10{11-12} Shells and one ch-1 sp.

Row 2: Work beginning Shell, work Shell in each Shell across to last Shell, (dc, ch 1, dc) in last Shell.

Repeat Row 2 until Back measures approximately 14{16-18}"/35.5{40.5-45.5} cm, ending by working a **wrong** side row.

Next Row: Work beginning Shell, work Shell in each Shell across; do **not** finish off: 11{12-13} Shells.

LEFT SLEEVE

Row 1: Ch 70, turn; 3 dc in fifth ch from hook, (skip next 4 chs, work Shell in next ch) 13 times, work Shell in each Shell across Back to last Shell, (dc, ch 1, dc) in last Shell: 24{25-26} Shells and one ch-1 sp.

Row 2: Work beginning Shell, work Shell in each Shell across to last Shell, dc in last Shell: 24{25-26} Shells.

Row 3: Ch 4, turn; work Shell in each Shell across to last Shell, dc in last Shell: 23{24-25} Shells and one ch-1 sp.

Row 4: Ch 4, turn; work Shell in each Shell across to last Shell, (dc, ch 1, dc) in last Shell, leave last ch-1 sp unworked: 22{23-24} Shells and 2 ch-1 sps.

Row 5: Work beginning Shell, work Shell in each Shell across to last Shell, (dc, ch 1, dc) in last Shell: 22{23-24} Shells and one ch-1 sp.

Rows 6-29: Repeat Rows 2-5, 6 times: 10{11-12} Shells and one ch-1 sp.

Rows 30 thru 34{35-36}: Repeat Row 5, 5{6-7} times.

Row 35{36-37}: Ch 1, turn; sc in first dc, (skip next ch-1 sp, sc in next 4 dc) across to last 2 ch-1 sps, skip next ch-1 sp, sc in next 3 dc, skip next dc and last ch-1 sp, sc in last dc: 41{45-49} sc.

Row 36{37-38}: Ch 1, turn; sc in each sc across; do **not** finish off.

EDGING

Do **not** turn; to begin working in rounds, slip st in first sc worked on last row.

Rnd 1: Ch 1, with **right** side facing, sc in each sc around working sc decrease 2{3-4} times evenly spaced; join with slip st to first sc: 39{42-45} sc.

When you join ribbon for the first time on Rnd 2, leave a long length that will be tacked to the wrong side. Do not cut ribbon at end of rounds; allow ribbon to hang on the right side and form a loop when beginning next ribbon round.

Rnd 2 (Joining ribbon)**:** Ch 1, do **not** turn; sc in same sc as joining, join ribbon with loop, (sc in next 3 sc, join ribbon with loop) around to last 2 sc, sc in last 2 sc; join with slip st to first sc.

Rnds 3 and 4: Ch 1, sc in each sc around; join with slip st to first sc.

Rnd 5: Repeat Rnd 2; cut ribbon.

Rnd 6: Ch 3, 2 dc in same sc as joining, skip next 2 sc, (3 dc in next sc, skip next 2 sc) around; join with slip st to top of beginning ch-3; finish off.

Whipstitch Sleeve seams ***(Fig. 11a, page 47)***.

RIGHT SLEEVE EDGING

Rnd 1: With **right** side of Right Sleeve facing, using larger size hook and working in free loops of beginning ch ***(Fig. 8, page 47)***, join yarn with slip st in first ch; ch 1, sc in same st and in each ch around working sc decrease 2{3-4} times evenly spaced; join with slip st to first sc: 39{42-45} sc.

Rnds 2-6: Work same as Left Sleeve Edging.

BODY EDGING

Rnd 1: With **right** side facing and using larger size hook, join yarn with slip st in Left Sleeve seam; ch 3, work 47{50-53} dc evenly spaced across bottom edge of Back, work 48{51-54} dc evenly spaced across Right Sleeve, work 42{45-48} dc evenly spaced across top edge of Back, work 48{51-54} dc evenly spaced across Left Sleeve; join with slip st to top of beginning ch-3: 186{198-210} sts.

Rnd 2 (Joining ribbon)**:** Ch 1, do **not** turn; sc in same st as joining, join ribbon with loop, (sc in next 3 dc, join ribbon with loop) around to last 2 dc, sc in last 2 dc; join with slip st to first sc, do **not** cut ribbon.

Rnds 3-6: Work same as Left Sleeve Edging.

Weave in all yarn ends.
Pull ribbon ends to wrong side and tack in place.✻

Child's Dress

INTERMEDIATE

Size	Finished Chest Measurement	
Small	21"	(53.5 cm)
Medium	23"	(58.5 cm)
Large	$25^1/_2$"	(65 cm)

Size Note: Instructions are written for size Small with sizes Medium and Large in braces { }. Instructions will be easier to read if you circle all the numbers pertaining to your child's size. If only one number is given, it applies to all sizes.

MATERIALS

100% Cotton Light Weight Variegated Yarn (LIGHT 3)
[1.75 ounces, 136 yards
(50 grams, 125 meters) per skein**]**:
4{6-7} skeins
Bulky Weight Ribbon Yarn (solid style) (BULKY 5)
[1.75 ounces, 80 yards
(50 grams, 73 meters) per ball**]**:1 ball
Crochet hook, size D (3.25 mm) **or** size needed for gauge

GAUGE: With light weight yarn, 20 dc and 10 rows = 4" (10 cm)

Gauge Swatch: 4" (10 cm) square
With light weight yarn, ch 22.
Row 1: Dc in fourth ch from hook **(3 skipped chs count as first dc)** and in each ch across: 20 dc.
Rows 2-10: Ch 3 **(counts as first dc)**, turn; dc in next dc and in each dc across.
Finish off.

JOINING RIBBON WITH DC

To insert the hook through the ribbon at the same distance without measuring each time, push the loop on the hook about $1^3/_4$" (4.5 cm) from the tip (near the center of the finger hold). Using this as a guide, insert the hook through the center of the ribbon at this length ***(Figs. 2a & b, page 6)***.

Joining ribbon in front: YO, insert hook through ribbon, then in next dc and complete dc ***(Figs. 6a-c, page 10)***.

Joining ribbon in back: YO, insert hook in next dc then through ribbon, and complete dc ***(Figs. 6d & e, page 10)***.

FRONT

With light weight yarn, ch 71{78-85} **loosely**.

Row 1 (Right side)**:** Sc in second ch from hook and in each ch across: 70{77-84} sc.

Note: Loop a short piece of yarn around any stitch to mark Row 1 as **right** side.

Row 2: Ch 1, turn; sc in each sc across.

When you join ribbon for the first time on Row 3, leave a long length that will be tacked to the wrong side. Do not cut ribbon at end of rows; allow ribbon to hang on the right side and form a loop when beginning next ribbon row.

Row 3 (Joining ribbon)**:** Ch 3 **(counts as first dc, now and throughout)**, turn; dc in next 1{2-1} st(s), (dc in next st joining ribbon in **front**, dc in next st) across.

Row 4 (Joining ribbon)**:** Ch 3, turn; (dc in next st, dc in next st joining ribbon in **back**) across to last 1{2-1} st(s), dc in last 1{2-1} st(s).

Rows 5-8: Repeat Rows 3 and 4 twice.

Row 9: Ch 3, turn; dc in next 9{10-11} dc, skip next 2 dc, (2 dc, ch 1, 2 dc) in next dc, ★ skip next 2 dc, dc in next 4{5-6} dc, skip next 2 dc, (2 dc, ch 1, 2 dc) in next dc; repeat from ★ 4 times **more**, skip next 2 dc, dc in last 10{11-12} dc: 64{71-78} dc and 6 ch-1 sps.

Instructions continued on page 32.

Rows 10 thru 12{14-16}: Ch 3, turn; dc in next 9{10-11} dc, skip next 2 dc, (2 dc, ch 1, 2 dc) in next ch-1 sp, ★ skip next 2 dc, dc in next 4{5-6} dc, skip next 2 dc, (2 dc, ch 1, 2 dc) in next ch-1 sp; repeat from ★ 4 times **more**, skip next 2 dc, dc in last 10{11-12} dc.

BODY SHAPING

Rows 1-6 (Decrease rows)**:** Ch 3, turn; dc in next dc and in each dc across to within 2 dc of next ch-1 sp, skip next 2 dc, (2 dc, ch 1, 2 dc) in next ch-1 sp, ★ skip next 2 dc, dc in next 4{5-6} dc, skip next 2 dc, (2 dc, ch 1, 2 dc) in next ch-1 sp; repeat from ★ 4 times **more**, skip next 2 dc, dc in each dc across to last dc, leave last dc unworked: 58{65-72} dc and 6 ch-1 sps.

Rows 7 and 8: Ch 3, turn; dc in next dc and in each dc across to within 2 dc of next ch-1 sp, skip next 2 dc, (2 dc, ch 1, 2 dc) in next ch-1 sp, ★ skip next 2 dc, dc in next 4{5-6} dc, skip next 2 dc, (2 dc, ch 1, 2 dc) in next ch-1 sp; repeat from ★ 4 times **more**, skip next 2 dc, dc in each dc across.

Rows 9 and 10 (Decrease rows)**:** Ch 3, turn; dc in next dc and in each dc across to within 2 dc of next ch-1 sp, skip next 2 dc, (2 dc, ch 1, 2 dc) in next ch-1 sp, ★ skip next 2 dc, dc in next 4{5-6} dc, skip next 2 dc, (2 dc, ch 1, 2 dc) in next ch-1 sp; repeat from ★ 4 times **more**, skip next 2 dc, dc in each dc across to last dc, leave last dc unworked: 56{63-70} dc and 6 ch-1 sps.

Rows 11 thru 18{22-22}: Repeat Rows 7-10, 2{3-3} times: 52{57-64} dc and 6 ch-1 sps.

Rows 19{23-23} thru 20{26-28}: Ch 3, turn; dc in next 3{3-4} dc, skip next 2 dc, (2 dc, ch 1, 2 dc) in next ch-1 sp, ★ skip next 2 dc, dc in next 4{5-6} dc, skip next 2 dc, (2 dc, ch 1, 2 dc) in next ch-1 sp; repeat from ★ 4 times **more**, skip next 2 dc, dc in last 4{4-5} dc.

ARMHOLE SHAPING

Row 1: Turn; skip first dc, slip st in next 3{3-4} dc, ch 3, skip next 2 dc, (2 dc, ch 1, 2 dc) in next ch-1 sp, ★ skip next 2 dc, dc in next 4{5-6} dc, skip next 2 dc, (2 dc, ch 1, 2 dc) in next ch-1 sp; repeat from ★ 4 times **more**, skip next 2 dc, dc in next dc, leave remaining sts unworked: 46{51-56} dc and 6 ch-1 sps.

Row 2: Ch 3, turn; skip next 2 dc, 3 dc in next ch-1 sp, skip next 2 dc, dc in next 4{5-6} dc, ★ skip next 2 dc, (2 dc, ch 1, 2 dc) in next ch-1 sp, skip next 2 dc, dc in next 4{5-6} dc; repeat from ★ 3 times **more**, skip next 2 dc, 3 dc in next dc, leave remaining sts unworked: 43{48-53} dc and 4 ch-1 sps.

Row 3: Turn; skip first dc, slip st in next dc, ch 3, dc in next 5{6-7} dc, skip next 2 dc, (2 dc, ch 1, 2 dc) in next ch-1 sp, ★ skip next 2 dc, dc in next 4{5-6} dc, skip next 2 dc, (2 dc, ch 1, 2 dc) in next ch-1 sp; repeat from ★ 2 times **more**, skip next 2 dc, dc in last 6{7-8} dc: 40{45-50} dc and 4 ch-1 sps.

Rows 4-7: Ch 3, turn; dc in next 5{6-7} dc, skip next 2 dc, (2 dc, ch 1, 2 dc) in next ch-1 sp, ★ skip next 2 dc, dc in next 4{5-6} dc, skip next 2 dc, (2 dc, ch 1, 2 dc) in next ch-1 sp; repeat from ★ 2 times **more**, skip next 2 dc, dc in last 6{7-8} dc.

NECK SHAPING - FIRST SIDE

Row 1: Ch 3, turn; dc in next 5{6-7} dc, skip next 2 dc, (2 dc, ch 1, 2 dc) in next ch-1 sp, skip next 2 dc, dc in next 4{5-6} dc, leave remaining sts unworked: 14{16-18} dc and one ch-1 sp.

Row 2: Turn; skip first dc, slip st in next 2{3-3} dc, ch 3, dc in next 1{1-2} dc, skip next 2 dc, (2 dc, ch 1, 2 dc) in next ch-1 sp, skip next 2 dc, dc in last 6{7-8} dc: 12{13-15} dc and one ch-1 sp.

Row 3: Ch 3, turn; dc in next 5{6-7} dc, skip next 2 dc, (2 dc, ch 1, 2 dc) in next ch-1 sp, leave remaining sts unworked: 10{11-12} dc and one ch-1 sp.

Row 4: Turn; skip first dc, slip st in next dc and in next ch-1 sp, ch 3, 2 dc in same sp, skip next 2 dc, dc in last 6{7-8} dc: 9{10-11} dc.

Row 5: Ch 3, turn; dc in next 7{8-9} dc, leave remaining dc unworked: 8{9-10} dc.

Sizes Medium and Large - last {1-2} row(s): Ch 3, turn; dc in next dc and in each dc across.

Finish off.

NECK SHAPING - SECOND SIDE

Row 1: With **wrong** side facing, skip 2 ch-1 sps and next 2 dc from First Side, join yarn with slip st in next dc; ch 3, dc in next 3{4-5} dc, skip next 2 dc, (2 dc, ch 1, 2 dc) in next ch-1 sp, skip next 2 dc, dc in last 6{7-8} dc: 14{16-18} dc and one ch-1 sp.

Row 2: Ch 3, turn; dc in next 5{6-7} dc, skip next 2 dc, (2 dc, ch 1, 2 dc) in next ch-1 sp, skip next 2 dc, dc in next 2{2-3} dc, leave remaining sts unworked: 12{13-15} dc and one ch-1 sp.

Row 3: Turn; skip first dc, slip st in next 3{3-4} dc and in next ch-1 sp, ch 3, (dc, ch 1, 2 dc) in same sp, dc in last 6{7-8} dc: 10{11-12} dc and one ch-1 sp.

Row 4: Ch 3, turn; dc in next 5{6-7} dc, skip next 2 dc, 3 dc in next ch-1 sp, leave remaining sts unworked: 9{10-11} dc.

Row 5: Turn; skip first dc, slip st in next dc, ch 3, dc in last 7{8-9} dc: 8{9-10} dc.

Sizes Medium and Large - last {1-2} row(s): Ch 3, turn; dc in next dc and in each dc across.

Finish off.

BACK

Work same as Front.

FINISHING

Whipstitch shoulder and side seams ***(Fig. 11a, page 47)***.

ARMHOLE EDGING

Rnd 1: With **right** side facing, join yarn with slip st at underarm seam; ch 1, work 54{58-64} sc evenly spaced around armhole; join with slip st to first sc.

Rnds 2 and 3 (Joining ribbon)**:** Ch 3, do **not** turn; dc in next st joining ribbon in **front**, (dc in next st, dc in next st joining ribbon in **front**) around; join with slip st to first dc.

Finish off.

NECK EDGING

Rnd 1: With **right** side facing, join yarn with slip st at shoulder seam; ch 1, work 68{78-88} sc evenly spaced around neck edge; join with slip st to first sc.

Rnds 2 and 3 (Joining ribbon)**:** Ch 3, do **not** turn; dc in next st joining ribbon in **front**, (dc in next st, dc in next st joining ribbon in **front**) around; join with slip st to first dc.

Finish off.

Weave in all yarn ends.
Pull ribbon ends to wrong side and tack in place.*

Shell

EASY

Size	Finished Bust Measurement
Small	30½" (77.5 cm)
Medium	35" (89 cm)
Large	39¼" (99.5 cm)
X-Large	43½" (110.5 cm)

Size Note: Instructions are written for size Small with sizes Medium, Large and X-Large in braces { }. Instructions will be easier to read if you circle all the numbers pertaining to your size. If only one number is given, it applies to all sizes.

MATERIALS

BULKY 5

- Bulky Weight Ribbon Yarn (solid style) **[**1.75 ounces, 110 yards (50 grams, 100 meters) per ball**]**: 2 balls
- 100% Cotton Thread, size 5 **[**191 yards (175 meters) per ball**]**: 6{6-8-8} balls
- Crochet hook, size E (3.5 mm) **or** size needed for gauge
- Steel crochet hook, size 6 (1.8 mm)
- Safety pin

GAUGE: With larger size hook and holding 2 strands of thread together, 22 dc and 10 rows = 4" (10 cm)

Gauge Swatch: 4" (10 cm) square
With larger size hook and holding 2 strands of thread together, ch 24.
Row 1: Dc in fourth ch from hook **(3 skipped chs count as first dc)** and in each ch across: 22 dc.
Rows 2-10: Ch 3 **(counts as first dc)**, turn; dc in next dc and in each dc across.
Finish off.

STITCH GUIDE

SMALL SHELL
(2 dc, ch 1, 2 dc) in st or ch-1 sp indicated.
LARGE SHELL
(3 dc, ch 1, 3 dc) in ch-1 sp indicated.

RIBBON FLOWER

To insert the hook through the ribbon at the same distance without measuring each time, push the loop on the hook about 1¾" (4.5 cm) from the tip (near the center of the finger hold). Using this as a guide, insert the hook through the center of the ribbon at this length ***(Figs. 2a & b, page 6)***.

Petals: Using smaller size hook ***(see Joining Ribbon and Changing Hook Size, page 4)***, insert hook through ribbon and push ribbon next to loop on hook, ★ insert hook back into same side of ribbon as you last came out of and push ribbon next to loop on hook; repeat from ★ 6 times **more**, with thread YO and draw through all ribbon holes leaving previous loop on hook: 2 loops on hook. Repeat Petals, 2 times **more**: 4 loops on hook. With thread, YO and draw through all 4 loops on hook ***(Figs. 3a-d, page 7)***, ch 1 to close.

Instructions continue on page 36.

BODICE

With larger size hook and holding two strands of thread together, ch 168{192-216-240} loosely; join with slip st to form a ring being careful not to twist ch.

Rnd 1: Ch 1, sc in same st as joining and in each ch around: 168{192-216-240} sc.

Rnd 2: Ch 3 **(counts as first dc, now and throughout)**, turn; dc in next st and in each st around; join with slip st to first dc.

Repeat Rnd 2 until Bodice measures approximately 4¼{4¾-5-5½}"/11{12-12.5-14} cm from beginning ch **or** to desired length.

BODY

Rnd 1: Ch 3, turn; dc in same st as joining, ch 2, skip next 3 dc, sc in next dc, ch 5, skip next 3 dc, sc in next dc, ch 2, skip next 3 dc, ★ work Small Shell in next dc, ch 2, skip next 3 dc, sc in next dc, ch 5, skip next 3 dc, sc in next dc, ch 2, skip next 3 dc; repeat from ★ around, 2 dc in same st as first dc, sc in top of first dc to form last ch-1 sp (Shell completed): 14{16-18-20} Small Shells.

Rnd 2: Ch 3, turn; dc in last sp made, ch 5, skip next ch-2 sp, sc in next ch-5 sp, ch 5, skip next ch-2 sp, ★ work Small Shell in next Shell (ch-1 sp), ch 5, skip next ch-2 sp, sc in next ch-5 sp, ch 5, skip next ch-2 sp; repeat from ★ around, 2 dc in same sp as first dc, sc in top of first dc to form last ch-1 sp.

Rnd 3: Ch 3, turn; dc in last sp made, ch 2, sc in next ch-5 sp, ch 5, sc in next ch-5 sp, ch 2, ★ work Small Shell in next Shell, ch 2, sc in next ch-5 sp, ch 5, sc in next ch-5 sp, ch 2; repeat from ★ around, 2 dc in same sp as first dc, sc in top of first dc to form last ch-1 sp.

Repeat Rnds 2 and 3 until Body measures approximately 7{7½-8-8½}"/18{19-20.5-21.5} cm, ending by working Rnd 3.

Next Rnd: Ch 3, turn; 2 dc in last sp made, ch 5, skip next ch-2 sp, sc in next ch-5 sp, ch 5, skip next ch-2 sp, ★ work Large Shell in next Shell, ch 5, skip next ch-2 sp, sc in next ch-5 sp, ch 5, skip next ch-2 sp; repeat from ★ around, 3 dc in same sp as first dc, sc in top of first dc to form last ch-1 sp.

Next Rnd (Right side)**:** Ch 3, turn; 2 dc in last sp made, ch 2, sc in next ch-5 sp, ch 5, sc in next ch-5 sp, ch 2, ★ work Large Shell in next Shell, ch 2, sc in next ch-5 sp, ch 5, sc in next ch-5 sp, ch 2; repeat from ★ around, 3 dc in same sp as first dc, sc in top of first dc to form last ch-1 sp.

Repeat last 2 rnds once.

Note: Loop a short piece of thread around any stitch to mark last rnd as **right** side.

Finish off.

FLOWER YOKE

Rnd 1: Since Rnd 1 is long, it has been broken down as follows:

Front: With **right** side facing, using larger size hook, holding one strand each of thread and ribbon together and working in free loops of beginning ch ***(Fig. 8, page 47)***, skip first 14{16-18-20} sts and join with slip st in next ch; ch 1, sc in same st, change to smaller size hook and make Ribbon Flower, change to larger size hook and holding thread and ribbon together, skip next 2 chs, sc in next ch, ★ (skip next ch, sc in next ch) 5{6-7-8} times, change to smaller size hook and make Ribbon Flower, change to larger size hook and holding thread and ribbon together, skip next 2 chs, sc in next ch; repeat from ★ 3 times **more**, (skip next ch, sc in next ch) 4 times.

Right Shoulder: Ch 1, change to smaller size hook and make Ribbon Flower, ★ change to larger size hook and holding thread and ribbon together, ch 7{8-8-9}, change to smaller size hook and make Ribbon Flower; repeat from ★ 4 times **more**, change to larger size hook and holding thread and ribbon together, ch 1.

Back: Skip next 12{16-20-24} chs (armhole), sc in next ch, (skip next ch, sc in next ch) 4 times, change to smaller size hook and make Ribbon Flower, change to larger size hook and holding thread and ribbon together, skip next 2 chs, sc in next ch, ★ (skip next ch, sc in next ch) 5{6-7-8} times, change to smaller size hook and make Ribbon Flower, change to larger size hook and holding thread and ribbon together, skip next 2 chs, sc in next ch; repeat from ★ 3 times **more**, (skip next ch, sc in next ch) 4 times.

Left Shoulder: Work same as Right Shoulder.

Remaining Front: Skip next 12{16-20-24} chs (armhole), (sc in next ch, skip next ch) 4 times; join with slip st to first sc.

You should have 5 Flowers on each Front and Back and 6 Flowers on each shoulder.

Rnd 2: ★ Slip st in back of next Flower, ch 6, change to smaller size hook and make Ribbon Flower, change to larger size hook and holding thread and ribbon together, ch 6; repeat from ★ around; join with slip st to first slip st; finish off.

Rnd 3: With **right** side facing, using larger size hook and holding one strand each of thread and ribbon together, join with slip st in back of any Flower, ★ ch 6{7-7-8}, slip st in back of next Flower; repeat from ★ around ending in same Flower as joining.

Rnd 4: ★ Ch 6, change to smaller size hook and make Ribbon Flower, change to larger size hook and holding thread and ribbon together, ch 6, slip st in back of next Flower; repeat from ★ around ending in same Flower as joining; finish off.

Rnd 5: With **right** side facing, using larger size hook and holding one strand each of thread and ribbon together, join with slip st in back of any Flower, ★ ch 5{6-6-7}, slip st in back of next Flower; repeat from ★ around ending in same Flower as joining; finish off.

TIE

With larger size hook and holding one strand each of thread and ribbon together, ch 1, change to smaller size hook and make Ribbon Flower, change to larger size hook and holding thread and ribbon together, chain a 42" (106.5 cm) length; cut thread and ribbon leaving a 45" (114.5 cm) length to work last Flower, slip loop from hook onto safety pin.

Weave Tie through Row 1 of Body beginning at center front.

Slip loop from safety pin onto smaller size hook, make Ribbon Flower; finish off.

Weave in all yarn ends.
Pull ribbon end from Rnd 1 of Yoke to wrong side and tack in place. Weave in remaining ribbon ends.*

Wrap Sweater

INTERMEDIATE

Size	Finished Bust Measurement
Small	30½" (77.5 cm)
Medium	34" (86.5 cm)
Large	37½" (95.5 cm)
X-Large	41½" (105.5 cm)

Size Note: Instructions are written for size Small with sizes Medium, Large and X-Large in braces { }. Instructions will be easier to read if you circle all the numbers pertaining to your size. If only one number is given, it applies to all sizes.

MATERIALS

Light Weight Yarn (LIGHT 3)
[2.5 ounces, 168 yards (70 grams, 154 meters) per skein]: 7{8-9-9} skeins
Super Bulky Weight Ribbon Yarn (SUPER BULKY 6) (checkerboard style)
[1.76 ounces, 28 yards (50 grams, 26 meters) per ball]:1 ball
Crochet hook, size H (5 mm) **or** size needed for gauge
Steel crochet hook, size 6 (1.8 mm)

GAUGE: With larger size hook and light weight yarn, in pattern, 5 V-sts and 8 rows = 3" (7.5 cm)

Gauge Swatch: 3½"w x 3¼"h (9 cm x 8.5 cm)
With larger size hook and light weight yarn, ch 19.
Row 1: Sc in second ch from hook and in each ch across: 18 sc.
Rows 2-9: Work same as Back Body Rows 1-8.
Finish off.

RIBBON FLOWER

Petals: Using smaller size hook ***(see Joining Ribbon and Changing Hook Size, page 4)*** and working in second row of holes, ★ skip 5 squares from loop on hook and insert hook through next hole on ribbon and slide previous loop on hook next to ribbon at tip of hook, with yarn, YO and pull up a loop through ribbon; repeat from ★ 5 times **more** keeping loops on hook close together, YO and draw through 6 yarn loops: one yarn loop and one combination loop. Repeat Petals 2 times **more**: 3 yarn loops and one combination loop. With yarn, YO and draw through all loops on hook, ch 1 to close ***(Figs. 4a-e, page 8)***.

RIBBON STITCH

Insert hook in st indicated, holding yarn and ribbon together, YO and pull up a loop, with yarn only, YO and draw through loops on hook.

BACK
EDGING

With larger size hook and light weight yarn, ch 79{88-97-106}.

Row 1 (Right side)**:** Sc in second ch from hook and in each ch across: 78{87-96-105} sc.

Note: Loop a short piece of yarn around any stitch to mark Row 1 as **right** side.

Row 2: Ch 1, turn; sc in each sc across.

Sizes Medium and X-Large Only: Repeat Row 2 twice.

BODY

Row 1: Ch 3 **(counts as first dc, now and throughout)**, turn; dc in next sc, ★ skip next 2 sc, (dc, ch 1, dc) in next sc; repeat from ★ across to last 4 sc, skip next 2 sc, dc in last 2 sc: 52{58-64-70} dc and 24{27-30-33} chs.

Note: Pattern is achieved by working into spaces **between** (dc, ch 1, dc) groups ***(Fig. 10, page 47)***.

Row 2: Ch 3, turn; skip next dc, (dc, ch 1, dc) in sp **before** next dc, ★ skip next 3 sts, (dc, ch 1, dc) in sp before next dc; repeat from ★ across to last 2 dc, skip next dc, dc in last dc: 52{58-64-70} dc and 25{28-31-34} chs.

Instructions continued on page 40.

Row 3: Ch 3, turn; dc in next dc, skip next 2 sts, (dc, ch 1, dc) in sp before next dc, ★ skip next 3 sts, (dc, ch 1, dc) in sp before next dc; repeat from ★ across to last 4 sts, skip next 2 sts, dc in last 2 dc: 52{58-64-70} dc and 24{27-30-33} chs.

Rows 4 thru 26{26-28-28}: Repeat Rows 2 and 3, 11{11-12-12} times, then repeat Row 2 once **more**.

ARMHOLE SHAPING

Row 1: Turn; skip first dc, slip st in next 3 sts, ch 3, dc in next dc, skip next 2 sts, (dc, ch 1, dc) in sp before next dc, ★ skip next 3 sts, (dc, ch 1, dc) in sp before next dc; repeat from ★ across to last 7 sts, skip next 2 sts, dc in next 2 dc, leave remaining sts unworked: 48{54-60-66} dc and 22{25-28-31} chs.

Row 2: Turn; skip first dc, slip st in next 4 sts, ch 3, dc in next dc, skip next 2 sts, (dc, ch 1, dc) in sp before next dc, ★ skip next 3 sts, (dc, ch 1, dc) in sp before next dc; repeat from ★ across to last 8 sts, skip next 2 sts, dc in next 2 dc, leave remaining sts unworked: 42{48-54-60} dc and 19{22-25-28} chs.

Row 3: Ch 3, turn; skip next dc, (dc, ch 1, dc) in sp before next dc, ★ skip next 3 sts, (dc, ch 1, dc) in sp before next dc; repeat from ★ across to last 2 dc, skip next dc, dc in last dc: 42{48-54-60} dc and 20{23-26-29} chs.

Row 4: Ch 3, turn; dc in next dc, skip next 2 sts, (dc, ch 1, dc) in sp before next dc, ★ skip next 3 sts, (dc, ch 1, dc) in sp before next dc; repeat from ★ across to last 4 sts, skip next 2 sts, dc in last 2 dc: 42{48-54-60} dc and 19{22-25-28} chs.

Repeat Rows 3 and 4 until Armholes measure approximately 7{7½-8-8½}"/18{19-20.5-21.5} cm, ending by working a **wrong** side row.

RIGHT NECK SHAPING

Row 1: Ch 3, turn; skip next dc, (dc, ch 1, dc) in sp before next dc, ★ skip next 3 sts, (dc, ch 1, dc) in sp before next dc; repeat from ★ 3{4-5-6} times **more**, skip next 2 sts, dc in next dc, leave remaining sts unworked: 12{14-16-18} dc and 5{6-7-8} chs.

Row 2: Ch 3, turn; dc in next dc, skip next 2 sts, (dc, ch 1, dc) in sp before next dc, ★ skip next 3 sts, (dc, ch 1, dc) in sp before next dc; repeat from ★ across to last 4 sts, skip next 2 sts, dc in last 2 dc; finish off: 12{14-16-18} dc and 4{5-6-7} chs.

LEFT NECK SHAPING

Row 1: With **right** side facing, skip 9{10-11-12} ch-1 sps and next dc from Right Neck and join yarn with slip st in next dc, ch 3, skip next 2 sts, (dc, ch 1, dc) in sp before next dc, ★ skip next 3 sts, (dc, ch 1, dc) in sp before next dc; repeat from ★ across to last 2 dc, skip next dc, dc in last dc: 12{14-16-18} dc and 5{6-7-8} chs.

Row 2: Ch 3, turn; dc in next dc, skip next 2 sts, (dc, ch 1, dc) in sp before next dc, ★ skip next 3 sts, (dc, ch 1, dc) in sp before next dc; repeat from ★ across to last 4 sts, skip next 2 sts, dc in last 2 dc; finish off: 12{14-16-18} dc and 4{5-6-7} chs.

RIGHT FRONT

Work same as Back through Row 9{9-11-11} of Body.

NECK SHAPING

Row 1: Ch 3, turn; skip next dc, (dc, ch 1, dc) in sp before next dc, ★ skip next 3 sts, (dc, ch 1, dc) in sp before next dc; repeat from ★ across to last 7{8-9-10} ch-1 sps, leave remaining sts unworked: 37{41-45-49} dc and 18{20-22-24} chs.

Row 2: Turn; skip first dc, slip st in next 4 sts, ch 3, skip next dc, (dc, ch 1, dc) in sp before next dc, ★ skip next 3 sts, (dc, ch 1, dc) in sp before next dc; repeat from ★ across to last 4 sts, skip next 2 sts, dc in last 2 dc: 35{39-43-47} dc and 16{18-20-22} chs.

Row 3: Ch 3, turn; skip next dc, (dc, ch 1, dc) in sp before next dc, ★ skip next 3 sts, (dc, ch 1, dc) in sp before next dc; repeat from ★ across to last 7 sts, leave remaining sts unworked: 31{35-39-43} dc and 15{17-19-21} chs.

Row 4: Ch 3, turn; skip next 2 sts, (dc, ch 1, dc) in sp before next dc, ★ skip next 3 sts, (dc, ch 1, dc) in sp before next dc; repeat from ★ across to last 4 sts, skip next 2 sts, dc in last 2 dc: 31{35-39-43} dc and 14{16-18-20} chs.

Row 5: Ch 3, turn; skip next dc, (dc, ch 1, dc) in sp before next dc, ★ skip next 3 sts, (dc, ch 1, dc) in sp before next dc; repeat from ★ across to last 4 sts, leave remaining sts unworked: 29{33-37-41} dc and 14{16-18-20} chs.

Rows 6-17: Repeat Rows 4 and 5, 6 times: 17{21-25-29} dc and 8{10-12-14} chs.

ARMHOLE SHAPING

Rows 1 and 2: Ch 3, turn; skip next 2 sts, (dc, ch 1, dc) in sp before next dc, ★ skip next 3 sts, (dc, ch 1, dc) in sp before next dc; repeat from ★ across to last 4 sts, leave remaining sts unworked: 13{17-21-25} dc and 6{8-10-12} chs.

Instructions continued on page 42.

Row 3: Ch 3, turn; skip next 2 sts, (dc, ch 1, dc) in sp before next dc, ★ skip next 3 sts, (dc, ch 1, dc) in sp before next dc; repeat from ★ across to last 4 sts, dc in next dc, leave remaining sts unworked: 12{16-20-24} dc and 5{7-9-11} chs.

Sizes Medium, Large and X-Large Only
Row 4: Ch 3, turn; dc in next dc, skip next 2 sts, (dc, ch 1, dc) in sp before next dc, ★ skip next 3 sts, (dc, ch 1, dc) in sp before next dc; repeat from ★ across to last 4 sts, leave remaining sts unworked: {14-18-22} dc and {6-8-10} chs.

Row 5: Ch 3, turn; skip next 2 sts, (dc, ch 1, dc) in sp before next dc, ★ skip next 3 sts, (dc, ch 1, dc) in sp before next dc; repeat from ★ across to last 2 dc, skip next dc, dc in last dc.

Repeat Rows 4 and 5, {0-1-2} time(s) ***(see Zeros, page 47)***: {14-16-18} dc and {6-7-8} chs.

All Sizes
Row 4{6-8-10}: Ch 3, turn; dc in next dc, skip next 2 sts, (dc, ch 1, dc) in sp before next dc, ★ skip next 3 sts, (dc, ch 1, dc) in sp before next dc; repeat from ★ across to last 4 sts, skip next 2 sts, dc in last 2 dc: 12{14-16-18} dc and 4{5-6-7} chs.

Row 5{7-9-11}: Ch 3, turn; skip next dc, (dc, ch 1, dc) in sp before next dc, ★ skip next 3 sts, (dc, ch 1, dc) in sp before next dc; repeat from ★ across to last 2 dc, skip next dc, dc in last dc: 12{14-16-18} dc and 5{6-7-8} chs.

Repeat last 2 rows until Armhole measures same as Back, ending by working a **wrong** side row; finish off.

LEFT FRONT

Work same as Back through Row 9{9-11-11} of Body; finish off.

NECK SHAPING

Row 1: With **wrong** side facing, skip first 7{8-9-10} ch-1 sps and next dc and join yarn with slip st in sp before next dc; ch 3, dc in same sp, ★ skip next 3 sts, (dc, ch 1, dc) in sp before next dc; repeat from ★ across to last 2 dc, skip next dc, dc in last dc: 37{41-45-49} dc and 17{19-21-23} chs.

Row 2: Ch 3, turn; dc in next dc, skip next 2 sts, (dc, ch 1, dc) in sp before next dc, ★ skip next 3 sts, (dc, ch 1, dc) in sp before next dc; repeat from ★ across to last 5 sts, leave remaining sts unworked: 34{38-42-46} dc and 16{18-20-22} chs.

Row 3: Turn; skip first dc, slip st in next 3 sts, ch 3, skip next 2 sts, (dc, ch 1, dc) in sp before next dc, ★ skip next 3 sts, (dc, ch 1, dc) in sp before next dc; repeat from ★ across to last 2 dc, skip next dc, dc in last dc: 32{36-40-44} dc and 15{17-19-21} chs.

Row 4: Ch 3, turn; dc in next dc, skip next 2 sts, (dc, ch 1, dc) in sp before next dc, ★ skip next 3 sts, (dc, ch 1, dc) in sp before next dc; repeat from ★ across to last 4 sts, leave remaining sts unworked: 30{34-38-42} dc and 14{16-18-20} chs.

Row 5: Ch 3, turn; skip next 2 sts, (dc, ch 1, dc) in sp before next dc, ★ skip next 3 sts, (dc, ch 1, dc) in sp before next dc; repeat from ★ across to last 2 dc, skip next dc, dc in last dc.

Rows 6-17: Repeat Rows 4 and 5, 6 times: 18{22-26-30} dc and 8{10-12-14} chs.

ARMHOLE SHAPING

Row 1: Turn; skip first dc, slip st in next 3 sts, ch 3, (dc, ch 1, dc) in sp before next dc, ★ skip next 3 sts, (dc, ch 1, dc) in sp before next dc; repeat from ★ across to last 4 sts, leave remaining sts unworked: 15{19-23-27} dc and 7{9-11-13} chs.

Row 2: Ch 3, turn; skip next 2 sts, (dc, ch 1, dc) in sp before next dc, ★ skip next 3 sts, (dc, ch 1, dc) in sp before next dc; repeat from ★ across to last 4 sts, leave remaining sts unworked: 13{17-21-25} dc and 6{8-10-12} chs.

Row 3: Ch 3, turn; skip next 2 sts, (dc, ch 1, dc) in sp before next dc, ★ skip next 3 sts, (dc, ch 1, dc) in sp before next dc; repeat from ★ across to last 4 sts, leave remaining sts unworked: 11{15-19-23} dc and 5{7-9-11} chs.

Sizes Medium, Large and X-Large Only

Row 4: Ch 3, turn; skip next 2 sts, (dc, ch 1, dc) in sp before next dc, ★ skip next 3 sts, (dc, ch 1, dc) in sp before next dc; repeat from ★ across to last 4 sts, skip next 2 sts, dc in last 2 dc: {15-19-23} dc and {6-8-10} chs.

Row 5: Ch 3, turn; skip next dc, (dc, ch 1, dc) in sp before next dc, ★ skip next 3 sts, (dc, ch 1, dc) in sp before next dc; repeat from ★ across to last 4 sts, leave remaining sts unworked: {13-17-21} dc and {6-8-10} chs.

Repeat Rows 4 and 5, {0-1-2} time(s): {13-15-17} dc and {6-7-8} chs.

Instructions continued on page 44.

All Sizes
Row 4{6-8-10}: Ch 3, turn; dc in next ch, skip next dc, (dc, ch 1, dc) in sp before next dc, ★ skip next 3 sts, (dc, ch 1, dc) in sp before next dc; repeat from ★ across to last 4 sts, skip next 2 sts, dc in last 2 dc: 12{14-16-18} dc and 4{5-6-7} chs.

Row 5{7-9-11}: Ch 3, turn; skip next dc, (dc, ch 1, dc) in sp before next dc, ★ skip next 3 sts, (dc, ch 1, dc) in sp before next dc; repeat from ★ across to last 2 dc, skip next dc, dc in last dc: 12{14-16-18} dc and 5{6-7-8} chs.

Row 6{8-10-12}: Ch 3, turn; dc in next dc, skip next 2 sts, (dc, ch 1, dc) in sp before next dc, ★ skip next 3 sts, (dc, ch 1, dc) in sp before next dc; repeat from ★ across to last 4 sts, skip next 2 sts, dc in last 2 dc: 12{14-16-18} dc and 4{5-6-7} chs.

Repeat last 2 rows until Armhole measures same as Back, ending by working a **wrong** side row; finish off.

SLEEVE (Make 2)

EDGING

With larger size hook and light weight yarn, ch 37{40-43-46}.

Row 1 (Right side)**:** Sc in second ch from hook and in each ch across: 36{39-42-45} sc.

Note: Mark Row 1 as **right** side.

Row 2: Ch 1, turn; sc in each sc across.

BODY

Row 1: Ch 3, turn; dc in next sc, ★ skip next 2 sc, (dc, ch 1, dc) in next sc; repeat from ★ across to last 4 sc, skip next 2 sc, dc in last 2 sc: 24{26-28-30} dc and 10{11-12-13} chs.

Row 2: Ch 3, turn; skip next dc, (dc, ch 1, dc) in sp before next dc, ★ skip next 3 sts, (dc, ch 1, dc) in sp before next dc; repeat from ★ across to last 2 dc, skip next dc, dc in last dc: 24{26-28-30} dc and 11{12-13-14} chs.

Row 3: Ch 3, turn; dc in next dc, skip next 2 sts, (dc, ch 1, dc) in sp before next dc, ★ skip next 3 sts, (dc, ch 1, dc) in sp before next dc; repeat from ★ across to last 4 sts, skip next 2 sts, dc in last 2 dc: 24{26-28-30} dc and 10{11-12-13} chs.

Rows 4-6: Repeat Rows 2 and 3 once, then repeat Row 2 once **more**.

Row 7 (Increase row)**:** Ch 3, turn; (dc, ch 1, dc) in sp before next dc, ★ skip next 3 sts, (dc, ch 1, dc) in sp before next dc; repeat from ★ across to last dc, dc in last dc: 26{28-30-32} dc and 12{13-14-15} chs.

Row 8: Ch 3, turn; dc in next dc, skip next 2 sts, (dc, ch 1, dc) in sp before next dc, ★ skip next 3 sts, (dc, ch 1, dc) in sp before next dc; repeat from ★ across to last 4 sts, skip next 2 sts, dc in last 2 dc: 26{28-30-32} dc and 11{12-13-14} chs.

Row 9: Ch 3, turn; skip next dc, (dc, ch 1, dc) in sp before next dc, ★ skip next 3 sts, (dc, ch 1, dc) in sp before next dc; repeat from ★ across to last 2 dc, skip next dc, dc in last dc: 26{28-30-32} dc and 12{13-14-15} chs.

Rows 10-36: Repeat Rows 7-9, 9 times: 44{46-48-50} dc and 21{22-23-24} chs.

Repeat Rows 8 and 9 until Sleeve measures approximately 17{17¼-17½-17¾}"/ 43{44-44.5-45} cm from beginning ch, ending by working Row 9.

CAP

Row 1: Turn; skip first dc, slip st in next 4 sts, ch 3, skip next 2 sts, (dc, ch 1, dc) in sp before next dc, ★ skip next 3 sts, (dc, ch 1, dc) in sp before next dc; repeat from ★ across to last 7 sts, leave remaining sts unworked: 37{39-41-43} dc and 18{19-20-21} chs.

Row 2: Ch 3, turn; skip next 2 sts, (dc, ch 1, dc) in sp before next dc, ★ skip next 3 sts, (dc, ch 1, dc) in sp before next dc; repeat from ★ across to last 4 sts, leave remaining sts unworked: 35{37-39-41} dc and 17{18-19-20} chs.

Row 3: Ch 3, turn; dc in next ch, skip next dc, (dc, ch 1, dc) in sp before next dc, ★ skip next 3 sts, (dc, ch 1, dc) in sp before next dc; repeat from ★ across to last 4 sts, leave remaining sts unworked: 34{36-38-40} dc and 16{17-18-19} chs.

Row 4: Ch 3, turn; skip next 2 sts, (dc, ch 1, dc) in sp before next dc, ★ skip next 3 sts, (dc, ch 1, dc) in sp before next dc; repeat from ★ across to last 5 sts, leave remaining sts unworked: 31{33-35-37} dc and 15{16-17-18} chs.

Row 5: Ch 3, turn; skip next 2 sts, (dc, ch 1, dc) in sp before next dc, ★ skip next 3 sts, (dc, ch 1, dc) in sp before next dc; repeat from ★ across to last dc, dc in last dc: 32{34-36-38} dc and 15{16-17-18} chs.

Row 6: Ch 3, turn; skip next 3 sts, (dc, ch 1, dc) in sp before next dc, ★ skip next 3 sts, (dc, ch 1, dc) in sp before next dc; repeat from ★ across to last 4 sts, skip next 3 sts, dc in last dc: 30{32-34-36} dc and 14{15-16-17} chs.

Row 7: Ch 3, turn; dc in next dc, skip next 2 sts, (dc, ch 1, dc) in sp before next dc, ★ skip next 3 sts, (dc, ch 1, dc) in sp before next dc; repeat from ★ across to last 4 sts, skip next 2 sts, dc in last 2 dc: 30{32-34-36} dc and 13{14-15-16} chs.

Row 8: Ch 3, turn; skip next 4 sts, (dc, ch 1, dc) in sp before next dc, ★ skip next 3 sts, (dc, ch 1, dc) in sp before next dc; repeat from ★ across to last 5 sts, skip next 4 sts, dc in last dc: 26{28-30-32} dc and 12{13-14-15} chs.

Repeat Rows 7 and 8, 3{3-4-4} times; then repeat Row 7 once **more**: 14{16-14-16} dc and 5{6-5-6} chs.

Finish off.

FINISHING

Whipstitch shoulder seams ***(Fig. 11a, page 47)***.

Sew Sleeves to Sweater, matching center of last row on Sleeve Cap to shoulder seam.

Whipstitch underarm and side in one continuous seam.

FLOWER TRIM

Row 1: With **right** side facing and larger size hook, join light weight yarn with slip st in Right Front corner on Row 1 of Edging; ch 1, work 16{16-19-19} sc evenly spaced across to shaping, work 88{92-96-100} sc evenly spaced across Right Front, work 29{32-35-38} sc evenly spaced across Back neck edge, work 87{91-95-99} sc evenly spaced across Left Front to bottom of shaping, work 16{16-19-19} sc evenly spaced across to bottom edge: 236{247-264-275} sc.

Row 2: Ch 1, turn; sc in each sc across.

Row 3 (Flower row)**:** Ch 1, turn; sc in first 16{16-19-19} sc, change to smaller size hook and leaving a 14{15-16-17}"/35.5{38-40.5-43} cm length for tie, make Ribbon Flower, ★ change to larger size hook, skip next 3 sc, sc in next 2 sc, work ribbon stitch, sc in next 2 sc, change to smaller size hook and make Ribbon Flower; repeat from ★ 17{18-19-20} times **more**, change to larger size hook, skip next 3 sc, (sc in next 2 sc, work ribbon stitch) across to last 16{16-19-19} sc, sc in each sc across; finish off leaving a 26{27-28-29}"/66{68.5-71-73.5} cm length for tie.

Attach a second length of ribbon in same st. Insert ties on Left Front into seam on Right Front. Bring ties around the Back and placing Right Front over Left Front, tie ribbons in a bow at side.

General INSTRUCTIONS

ABBREVIATIONS

ch(s)	chain(s)
cm	centimeters
dc	double crochet(s)
mm	millimeters
Rnd(s)	Round(s)
sc	single crochet(s)
sp(s)	space(s)
st(s)	stitch(es)
YO	yarn over

★ — work instructions following ★ as many **more** times as indicated in addition to the first time.

( ) or **[ ]** — work enclosed instructions as many times as specified by the number immediately following **or** work all enclosed instructions in the stitch or space indicated **or** contains explanatory remarks.

colon (:) — the number(s) given after a colon at the end of a row or round denote(s) the number of stitches or spaces you should have on that row or round.

CROCHET TERMINOLOGY		
UNITED STATES		INTERNATIONAL
slip stitch (slip st)	=	single crochet (sc)
single crochet (sc)	=	double crochet (dc)
half double crochet (hdc)	=	half treble crochet (htr)
double crochet (dc)	=	treble crochet(tr)
treble crochet (tr)	=	double treble crochet (dtr)
double treble crochet (dtr)	=	triple treble crochet (ttr)
triple treble crochet (tr tr)	=	quadruple treble crochet (qtr)
skip	=	miss

Yarn Weight Symbol & Names	LACE 0	SUPER FINE 1	FINE 2	LIGHT 3	MEDIUM 4	BULKY 5	SUPER BULKY 6
Type of Yarns in Category	Fingering, 10-count crochet thread	Sock, Fingering Baby	Sport, Baby	DK, Light Worsted	Worsted, Afghan, Aran	Chunky, Craft, Rug	Bulky, Roving
Crochet Gauge* Ranges in Single Crochet to 4" (10 cm)	32-42 double crochets**	21-32 sts	16-20 sts	12-17 sts	11-14 sts	8-11 sts	5-9 sts
Advised Hook Size Range	Steel*** 6,7,8 Regular hook B-1	B-1 to E-4	E-4 to 7	7 to I-9	I-9 to K-10.5	K-10.5 to M-13	M-13 and larger

*GUIDELINES ONLY: The chart above reflects the most commonly used gauges and hook sizes for specific yarn categories.

** Lace weight yarns are usually crocheted on larger-size hooks to create lacy openwork patterns. Accordingly, a gauge range is difficult to determine. Always follow the gauge stated in your pattern.

*** Steel crochet hooks are sized differently from regular hooks–the higher the number the smaller the hook, which is the reverse of regular hook sizing.

CROCHET HOOKS													
U.S.	B-1	C-2	D-3	E-4	F-5	G-6	H-8	I-9	J-10	K-10½	N	P	Q
Metric - mm	2.25	2.75	3.25	3.5	3.75	4	5	5.5	6	6.5	9	10	15

STEEL CROCHET HOOKS																
U.S.	00	0	1	2	3	4	5	6	7	8	9	10	11	12	13	14
Metric - mm	3.5	3.25	2.75	2.25	2.1	2	1.9	1.8	1.65	1.5	1.4	1.3	1.1	1	.85	.75

BEGINNER	Projects for first-time crocheters using basic stitches. Minimal shaping.
EASY	Projects using yarn with basic stitches, repetitive stitch patterns, simple color changes, and simple shaping and finishing.
INTERMEDIATE	Projects using a variety of techniques, such as basic lace patterns or color patterns, mid-level shaping and finishing.
EXPERIENCED	Projects with intricate stitch patterns, techniques and dimension, such as non-repeating patterns, multi-color techniques, fine threads, small hooks, detailed shaping and refined finishing.

GAUGE

Exact gauge is **essential** for proper size or fit. Before beginning your project, make the sample swatch given in the individual instructions using the hook specified. After completing the swatch, measure it, counting your stitches and rows carefully. If your swatch is larger or smaller than specified, make another, changing hook size to get the correct gauge. Keep trying until you find the size hook that will give you the specified gauge.

ZEROS

To consolidate the length of an involved pattern, zeros are sometimes used so that all sizes can be combined. For example, repeat Rows 4 and 5, {0-1-2} time(s) means the smallest size would do nothing, the second size would repeat Rows 4 and 5 once and the largest size would repeat Rows 4 and 5 twice.

FREE LOOPS OF A CHAIN

When instructed to work in free loops of a chain, work in loop indicated by arrow ***(Fig. 8)***.

Fig. 8

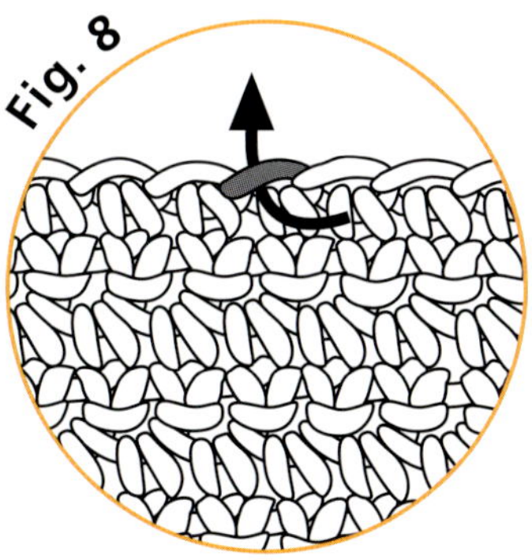

BACK OR BOTH LOOPS

Work only in loop(s) indicated by arrow ***(Fig. 9)***.

Fig. 9

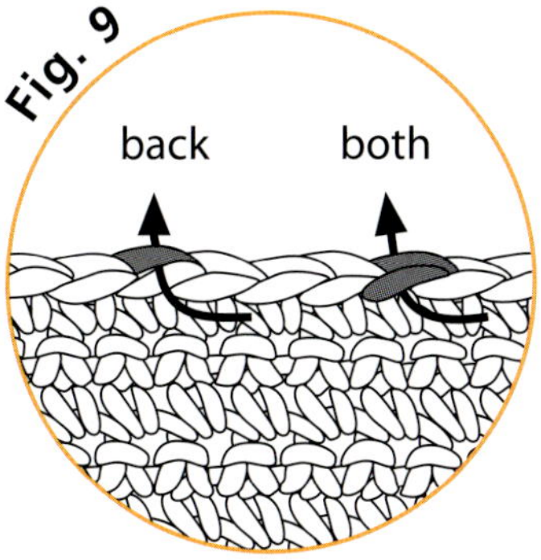

WORKING IN SPACE BEFORE A STITCH

When instructed to work in space **before** a stitch or in spaces **between** stitches, insert hook in space indicated by arrow ***(Fig. 10)***.

Fig. 10

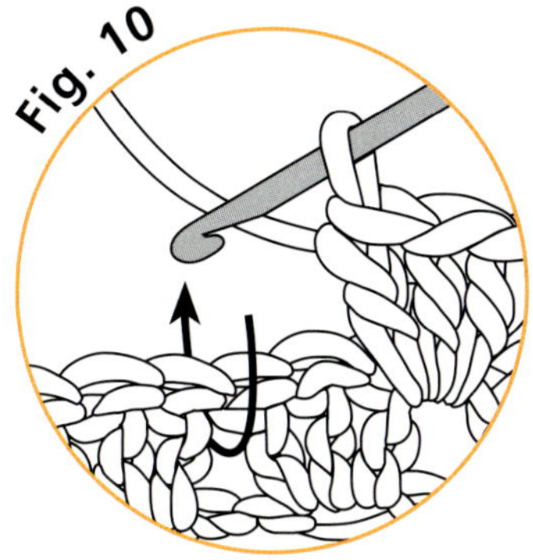

WHIPSTITCH

With **wrong** sides together, sew through both pieces once to secure the beginning of the seam, leaving an ample yarn end to weave in later. Insert the needle from **front** to **back** through two strands on each piece ***(Fig. 11a)*** **or** through inside loops only of stitches across Squares ***(Fig. 11b)***. Bring the needle around and insert it from **front** to **back** through the next strand(s) on both pieces. Repeat along the edge.

Fig. 11a

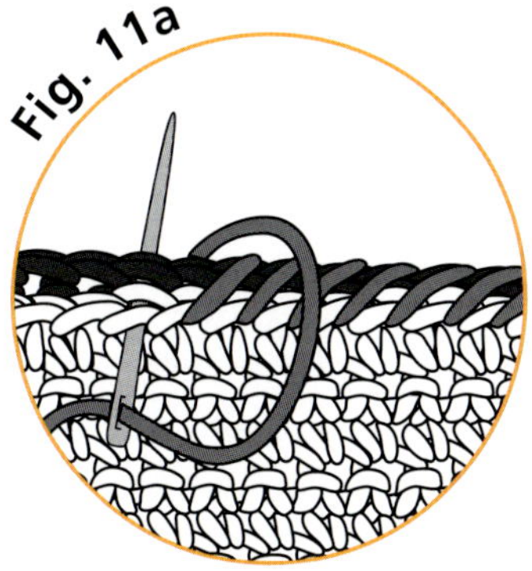

Fig. 11b

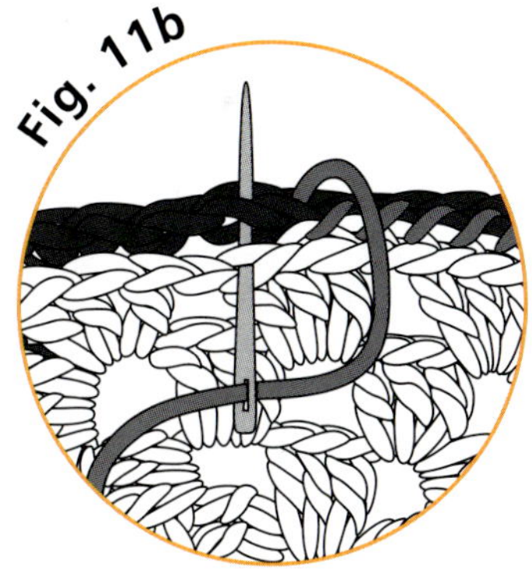

STRINGING BEADS

Thread a tapestry needle with the cut ends of a doubled length of sewing thread, leaving a loop at the opposite end. Slip the end of crochet thread through the loop. Slip the beads onto the needle and crochet thread ***(Fig. 12)***.

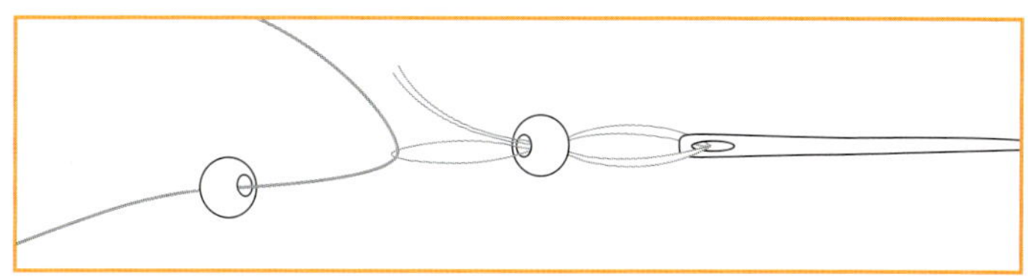

Yarn & Ribbon INFORMATION

The items in this leaflet were made using yarn, size 5 thread and various ribbons. Any brand may be used. It is best to refer to the yardage/meters when determining how many balls or skeins to purchase. Remember, to achieve the same look, it is the weight of yarn and type of ribbon that is important, not the brand.

For your convenience, listed below are the specific yarns, threads and ribbons used to create our photography models.

NECKLACE
Lion Brand® Incredible
#204 Accent on Black
Coats® Opera™, size 5
#501 Black

HAT
Lion Brand® Microspun
#124 Mocha
Crystal Palace Yarn, "Choo-Choo"
#2746 Toasted Marshmallow
Coats® Opera™, size 5
#560 Russet

SCARF
Moda Dea™ Spellbound™
2732 Wizard
Coats® Opera™, size 5
#560 Russet

PILLOW
Patons® Grace
#60012 Taupe
Crystal Palace Yarn "Deco Ribbon"
#9542 Dreamy

PURSE
Red Heart® Soft Yarn™
#4422 Tangerine
Offray Woven Ribbon,
Art. #S2353

BLANKET
Caron® Simply Soft®
#9703 Bone
Sheer Creations Wired Ribbon,
Item #1697937SC

TRIANGULAR SHAWL
Caron® Pizazz
#0004 Dusk
Coats® Opera™, size 5
#501 Black

BOLERO
Lion Brand® Microspun
#153 Ebony
Sheer Creations Ribbon,
Art. S23675

CHILD'S DRESS
Patons® Grace
#60901 Tangelo
Crystal Palace Yarn "Deco Ribbon"
#9234 Orange Crush

SHELL
Lion Brand® Incredible
#211 Emerald Isle
Coats® Opera™, size 5
#558 Teal

WRAP SWEATER
Lion Brand® Microspun
#134 Leaf
Caron® Pizazz
#0005 Meadow

PRODUCTION TEAM:
Technical Writer/Editor - Cathy Hardy • Editorial Writer - Susan McManus Johnson • Senior Graphic Artist - Lora Puls • Graphic Artist - Amy Temple • Photo Stylist - Cora Brown • Photographers - Mark Mathews and Jason Masters

We have made every effort to ensure that these instructions are accurate and complete. We cannot, however, be responsible for human error, typographical mistakes, or variations in individual work.